Reflections on Critical Museology

T0384933

Reflections on Critical Museology: Inside and Outside Museums offers a reflective and reflexive re-assessment of museum studies and the first wide-ranging account of critical museology.

Drawing on an extensive range of examples from museums and across the museological literature, which are purposefully representative of very different cultural backgrounds, the book issues a plea for critical thinking in and about museums. The various institutions covered and the plural analytical standpoints offer a broad interdisciplinary approach by intermingling art history, anthropology, sociocultural theories and heritage studies. The result is not claimed as a universal or all-encompassing account but a subjective review produced by J. Pedro Lorente, an art critic and historian who has been writing extensively about 'critical museology' in different languages for many years. Lorente offers a fascinating synopsis of his ideas in this extremely valuable short book, looking inside and outside museums, combining practice and theory, while also relating both to the work of museum professionals and to a range of publications by academics, including those from other research fields.

Reflections on Critical Museology: Inside and Outside Museums will be essential reading for university students and academics working in museum studies and cognate disciplines, such as art history, anthropology and cultural studies.

J. Pedro Lorente is Professor of Art History and Director of the MA in Museum Education and Communication at the University of Saragossa (Spain). He is the author of other books published by Routledge, such as *The Museums of Contemporary Art. Notion and Development* (also available in Spanish, French and Turkish editions) or *Public Art and Museums in Cultural Districts* (also available in Spanish version).

Museums in Focus
Series Editor: Kylie Message,
Australian National University, Australia

Committed to the articulation of big, even risky ideas, in small format publications, 'Museums in Focus' challenges authors and readers to experiment with, innovate, and press museums and the intellectual frameworks through which we view these. It offers a platform for approaches that radically rethink the relationships between cultural and intellectual dissent and crisis and debates about museums, politics and the broader public sphere.

'Museums in Focus' is motivated by the intellectual hypothesis that museums are not innately 'useful', safe' or even 'public' places and that recalibrating our thinking about them might benefit from adopting a more radical and oppositional form of logic and approach. Examining this problem requires a level of comfort with (or at least tolerance of) the idea of crisis, dissent, protest and radical thinking, and authors might benefit from considering how cultural and intellectual crisis, regeneration and anxiety have been dealt with in other disciplines and contexts.

The following list includes only the most-recent titles to publish within the series. A list of the full catalogue of titles is available at: www.routledge.com/Museums-in-Focus/book-series/MIF

Reflections on Critical Museology
Inside and Outside Museums
J. Pedro Lorente

Self-Determined First Nations Museums and Colonial Contestation
The Keeping Place
Robert Hudson and Shannon Woodcock

⌐MUSEUMS IN FOCUS⌐

Logo by James Verdon (2017)

Reflections on Critical Museology
Inside and Outside Museums

J. Pedro Lorente

Routledge
Taylor & Francis Group

LONDON AND NEW YORK

First published 2022
by Routledge
4 Park Square, Milton Park, Abingdon, Oxon OX14 4RN

and by Routledge
605 Third Avenue, New York, NY 10158

Routledge is an imprint of the Taylor & Francis Group, an informa business

British Library Cataloguing-in-Publication Data
A catalogue record for this book is available from the British Library

Library of Congress Cataloging-in-Publication Data
Title: Reflections on critical museology : inside and outside
    museums / J. Pedro Lorente. Other titles: Inside and outside
    museums
Description: Abingdon, Oxon ; New York, NY : Routledge, 2022. |
    Series: Museums in focus | Includes bibliographical references
    and index.
Identifiers: LCCN 2021058825 (print) | LCCN 2021058826
    (ebook) | ISBN 9781032202907 (hbk) | ISBN 9781032202952
    (pbk) | ISBN 9781003263050 (ebk)
Subjects: LCSH: Museums—Philosophy. | Museum techniques—
    Philosophy.
Classification: LCC AM7 .L595 2022 (print) | LCC AM7 (ebook) |
    DDC 069.01—dc23/eng/20220119
LC record available at https://lccn.loc.gov/2021058825
LC ebook record available at https://lccn.loc.gov/2021058826

ISBN: 978-1-032-20290-7 (hbk)
ISBN: 978-1-032-20295-2 (pbk)
ISBN: 978-1-003-26305-0 (ebk)

DOI: 10.4324/9781003263050

Typeset in Times New Roman
by Apex CoVantage, LLC

Anonymous graffiti, Athens. Image and logo by James Verdon (2017).

Contents

Illustrations

Introduction

This is a very short book, but one written over a long time. It has been hard work to produce this personal synthesis on one of my dearest topics, one which I have reconsidered over and over again while my thoughts gradually evolved in relation to my initial postulates, with no major changes in the essential arguments. For years, I have been explaining in my classes and public forums my conception of 'critical museology', by pointing out the intrinsic diversity of viewpoints in interpreting this trend that, since the turn of the millennium, has stirred up museum studies across the world: if something characterises critical museologists, it is precisely our staunch individual standpoint, with little adherence to collectively assumed leaderships and ideologies. The expression 'critical museology' has been increasingly used by many people in different languages, albeit with distinct connotations, while some other authors propose various labels instead, some of which are probably better, such as 'reflective/reflexive museology'. Being so closely linked with art criticism, whose study I have regularly combined with that of museums and museology, it is not surprising that, in my case, I feel a particular predilection for an appellation that, as with dominoes, would allow me to interconnect by means of the same word two apparently different itineraries of my career. The work of art critics bears many similarities to that of those who analyse museums in publications or other forums; all in all, if they achieve great professional and social projection, both art criticism and museology manage to influence not only their object of study but also public opinion, with their influential expansive wave sometimes reaching even distant continents. However, 'to influence' is no longer a politically correct expression in the artistic field since Michael Baxandall denounced that it designates as a passive recipient someone who is, in fact, an active agent. Therefore, other verbs should preferably be used, such as to adapt, react and emulate. In the same way, when calibrating the impact of a trend in museology that began to make itself known on North American

DOI: 10.4324/9781003263050-1

Figure 0.1 Façade of the National Gallery of Modern and Contemporary Art in
Rome with bronze lions by Davide Rivalta and philosophical sen-
tence by Maria Zambrano: "Roots must trust in flowers" (Photograph:
Adriano Mura, provided by Galleria Nazionale d'Arte Moderna e
Contemporanea).

Source: Photo by Alessandro Garofalo, provided by Galleria Nazionale d'Arte Moderna e
Contemporanea

university campuses and on some British ones as well, but always rallying the flag of anti-colonialism, it seems pertinent to vindicate the contributions that emerge outside its initial territorial epicentres. Thus, the point of view of a critical museologist situated on the periphery should have no less legitimacy!

Having said this, I hasten to clarify that I have intended to offer a broad panorama here, which ranges from the closest samples to distant horizons where my vision will have been less clear. I have made an attempt to intermix references to authors and institutions from different cultural contexts by combining foreign examples and ideas tracked in copious readings with my own reflections and 'fieldwork' as a persistent museum visitor. My writing has been inspired by a pair of questions asked by Kylie Message in the first volume of the series 'Routledge Museums in Focus': 'How has museum studies responded to a changed critical museology and political landscape? How has our approach to writing critique changed in the face of our changed subject?' (Message, 2018: 47). Following her double suggestion, I have endeavoured to offer a concise review of conspicuous critical developments in museums and museology. As I have shown, these are not two separate poles but are interconnected in a feedback loop, insofar as many recent changes that have marked the museum's internal praxis have occurred in relation to the critical turn beyond its walls. This book attempts to rethink together museum theory and practice, interconnecting internal museum uses with mindsets in outer academic circles. Hence the title *Reflections on Critical Museology, Inside and Outside Museums*, inspired by a suggestive museological dictum, 'The inside as outside', proclaimed by Elaine Heumann Gurian about the role of museums in the public realm (Gurian, 2006: 105). Looking inside and outside museums characterises, in many ways, my most distinctive perspective as a cultural historian, also in relation to my other works on art in the public sphere, wherein there is no solution of continuity between museum interior areas and outdoors. It is no coincidence, therefore, the attention paid in this book to public space, both inside and outside museums, would correspond to a second meaning of the title. Moreover, a third one should still be considered, because a critical museology worthy of that qualification must challenge traditional disciplinary boundaries so as to reflect on museological thinking from broader perspectives. Therefore, in response to another challenge posed by Prof. Message, this publication aims to offer a reconsideration that works as a 'reflective and reflexive reassessment' of museum studies in today's society and from a historical position (Message, 2018: 74). Museologists should reframe a retrospective disciplinary revision from the far-reaching viewpoint of heritage studies, in a self-critical way.

Such metadiscursive approach, which since the boom of postmodernity is a very generalised feature in all disciplines, has provided the argumentative arrangement and the melodic structure of this essay with a pitching tone. The *leitmotif* reiterated with variable words in every chapter has been a metamuseological reflection that interrelates past and present, theory and practice. It may not be amiss to recall at this point, with a self-deprecating touch of humour, the famous assertion, often attributed to theoretical physicist Richard Feynman, that the philosophy of science is as useful for scientists as ornithology is for birds. Some sceptics believe that the benefits of museology for museums are the same as those obtained for birds from ornithology (Popadić, 2020: 13). In 1965, when Raymond Singleton created the Department of Museum Studies at the University of Leicester, he carefully chose this expression to emphasise that his priority was to offer professional training rather than museological theorising. Paradoxically, this English academic context eventually became a world leading institution in the production of thoughtful publications and doctoral theses, the first of which, defended in 1983, was entitled *Museology and Its Traditions*. Years later, when I was a doctoral student there, I read the expression 'critical museology' on its pages for the first time in my life. So it can be stated that this dissertation marked a crucial milestone for me. Its author, Lynne Teather, offered a balanced overview of both museum theory and practice from a historical perspective, something which was not the prevailing trend among adherents of the 'new museology'. Professor Deirdre Stam had a point when she reproached this new trend for preferring to project an imaginary future based on beautiful intangible metaphors, opposed to present/past museums and museology repeatedly disqualified, without firstly having worried too much about knowing their real situation or their history (Stam, 1993). We should not repeat such fallacious arguments of neo-museologists but learn from their many virtues, notably their idealistic enthusiasm and their social vocation, which they have transmitted to the museologists of the following generation. As proud descendants of our neo-museological parents, critical museologists are inevitably marked by an Oedipal relationship with them (Lorente, 2006).

For this reason, it was convenient to begin this book by taking a retrospective glance, and summarising in a few words the milestones and legacies of the 'new museology', by warning about some terminological muddles because only in relation to that previous tag – so polysemic – can we talk about what distinguishes – or not – 'critical museology'. I am not the only one who thinks this way, as seen in Chapter 1, when reviewing the variable nomenclature echoing this critical turn in a number of authors and specialised museological publications as almost all of them allude in contrast or as a parallelism to 'new museology'. Both labels have often been correlatively used and, indeed with no reference to the new-museological upheaval, nothing that came later could be explained (Grau Lobo, 2010; Padró, 2010), as observed in the museum studies literature and in accordance with the common view propagated in leading encyclopaedias.[1] I believe this is consonant with the historic account regularly transmitted in university classrooms, or at least this is what I have been stating for years at the University of Saragossa in the course entitled 'From the new museology to critical museology' in the MA in *Museum Education and Communication*.

To the students of this postgraduate degree, I always point out that the educational services of museums constitute the main anchor to put critical museology in lively practice. Thus, it is not by chance that 'critical pedagogy' is a cardinal argument of Chapter 2, which begins by paying a tribute to the artists who paved the way for it through the so-called institutional critique. One of its main exponents, Andrea Fraser, advocated to turn it around by producing instead 'an Institution of Critique', something which, in my opinion, is already materialised in every museum that has replaced celebratory accounts with questions, doubts, irony, controversy, and even self-criticism. Yet, self-questioning must also be applied to critical pedagogy/museology itself as its success has somehow led to a terminological 'institutionalization' process, insofar as we have already created a new cultural canon with reiterated buzzwords, ubiquitous today. Nonetheless, it is not so peremptory to express ourselves with jargon that identifies us with the critical turn that now triumphs in all disciplines because, perhaps, those who really contribute the most to 'critical museology' might be people who do not even adopt that designation. I often say that some colleagues are not aware of being critical museologists, like Molière's bourgeois gentleman who spoke prose without knowing it.

Beyond vocabulary issues, what really matters is to advocate for a museum and a museology that will open to public debate a plurality of subjective points of view. Museums and exhibitions have always been spaces for interactions between different people and ideas, a ferment of conversations like those that emerged from the commentary on books and the press in cafes, clubs and gatherings where, according to Habermas, the modern public sphere developed. It is no less true that they have also traditionally worked as temples dedicated to the evangelisation of ideas and ideologies emanating from power. It is the eternal dilemma between temple and forum evoked by Duncan Cameron in a classic text of museum studies (Cameron, 1971). Yet, it seems that in our day the balance leans more towards making the museum an agora of dialectical interaction. This is the topic of Chapter 3, where I explain how the crisis of modernity broke with the homogeneous architectural paradigms that once prevailed and the museographical prototype of the 'white cube', which imposed a path favouring the initiatory assimilation of hegemonic cultural dogmas. By transferring to museology, some of Jacques Rancière's ideas from his 2008 book *Le spectateur éman-cipé*, I have attempted to highlight how visitors are now playing a proactive and self-conscious role in interpretation processes with the mediation of museum professionals, who are neither mere transmitters of an anonymous institutional discourse nor can be satisfied with vicariously reporting personal opinions through comments of third parties. The time has come to highlight the human criteria or dilemmas in both curatorship and museum studies, which should no longer exclusively be contents-focussed narratives but also reflections on museology/museography issues.

The corollary of this aspiration is that the museum must also direct our attention to itself and its evolution, especially when it has a strong historic identity. This is argued in Chapter 4, firstly with examples of museum devices and displays preserved or recovered as a testimony to the ways of seeing most typical of past times, kept in view – not always critically – for the sake of posterity; secondly, with reference to increasingly more museums that include, as integral part of the visit, some spaces in which they narrate – albeit in encomiastic terms – their institutional autobiography with words, images, and even with some historic pieces from the collection. My consideration that the museum's own memory is historic heritage worthy of being preserved and interpreted has been inspired by François Mairesse's exhortations on the leading role of History in the 'museal field' – an expression that combines terms from Pierre Bourdieu and Bernard Deloche – in a pioneering essay where he devoted an epigraph to the evolution from museology towards 'heritology' (Mairesse, 2006). By reconsidering that statement from a derivative point of view, which would be the transition from 'critical museology' towards 'critical heritage studies', I think that such a self-referential loop is even more justified, in which not only historic reflections are proposed but also a reflexion on these reflections.

It is often repeated that museums are institutions dedicated to memory. In Paris, this was symbolically represented in 1799, six years after the opening of a great public museum in the Louvre Palace, by installing in the garden in front of its entrance a Roman marble statue known as *Mnemosyne, Mother of the Muses*. I have often wondered if they placed this allegory of Memory facing the museum or the city. But it no longer matters much to me as my fundamental plea is that our museological reflection must cover what happens both inside and outdoors, including the museological postulates aired in classrooms, conferences, or publications of all kinds. To be consistent with that thesis, this book ends with some final (self-)critical reconsiderations by pointing out some of the shortcomings in every chapter or those ideas that should be reviewed and expanded from my point of view. I believe that this defence of a 'situated' personal perspective, which is a common factor in all my writings, is a primary characteristic of criticism and, therefore, of critical museology.

Nevertheless, even if this is a personal essay, it owes a lot to other people, starting with the students and interlocutors from whom I have learned so much, at either the University of Saragossa or other institutions where I have given talks on critical museology, at the invitation of colleagues to whom I am deeply indebted. It would be tedious to list all the names and events, but at least I allow myself to highlight one, which was for me especially endearing because of the dear comrades who arrived in good numbers from both sides of the Atlantic: the First International Symposium on Critical Museology, held in June 2011 by the Málaga Municipal Heritage Museum – Teresa Sauret being its director –, whose journal *Museo y Territorio* subsequently edited the proceedings – where Anthony Shelton published a preliminary version of his celebrated text 'Critical Museology: A Manifesto'. We were able to organise it thanks to the financial help of the Spanish Government with a subvention accorded by the Directorate General for Research, which has paid for successive research projects of which I have had the honour of being team leader (the one currently in force is: PGC2018–094351-B-C41). I have also received financial support for museum visits and publications through the budgets granted to the research group *Observatorio Aragonés de Arte en la Esfera Pública*, financed by the Government of Aragon with ERDF funds. Finally, I am indebted to the anonymous reviewers who examined my manuscript making useful suggestions and, most particularly, to Prof. Lynne Teather who has revised the final version. To all these academic companions and above all to my family, I wish to dedicate this book in the hope that I deserve their continuing support in the years to come.

Note

1 For example, Wikipedia, where 'critical museology' is always mentioned in relation to 'new museology': this happens in the long definition of *Museology* in both the English version, https://en.wikipedia.org/wiki/Museology, and the French one, https://fr.wikipedia.org/wiki/Mus%C3%A9ologie, but also in the Spanish edition, which already has a specific entry for 'Critical Museology' – not written by me – https://es.wikipedia.org/wiki/Museolog%C3%ADa_Cr%C3%ADtica#:~:text=La%20Museolog%C3%ADa%20Cr%C3%ADtica%20es%20una,y%20de%20la%20Nueva%20Museolog%C3%ADa (websites last consulted on 18 September 2021).

1 Academic echoes of the label 'critical museology' and its referents

Museología Crítica: temas selectos. Reflexiones desde la Cátedra William Bullock
—
Critical Museology: Selected Themes Reflections from the William Bullock Lecture Series

MU
×C

Figure 1.1 Cover of a book on critical museology published in 2019 by the MUAC-UNAM, México City.

DOI: 10.4324/9781003263050-2

1.1 Changing names for a shifting discipline: from 'new museology' to 'critical museology'

Treatises about museums were produced for centuries and some can be traced back to ancient times. The articulation of this branch of studies as a scientific discipline, with its own terminology, however, is relatively recent. It was a long time before an agreement was reached on a basic universal glossary with words like 'museology' or 'museography', first used in German and then in other languages, but not always with the same meanings, which changed considerably as the years went by (Waltz, 2018). It was not until the second half of the twentieth century when these two terms became standardised to respectively refer to museal theory and praxis (Klausewitz, 1989). Presumably, we owe this disambiguation to Jiri Neustupny and Jan Jelínek, who then developed a further taxonomical debate in their Czech language, culminated by another theoretician of great influence, Zbyněk Stránský, who proposed up to five categories: 'Historical museology', 'social museology', 'theoretical museology', 'applied museology' (museography) and 'special museology'.[1] Since then it would seem that the quest for qualifying adjectives for museology has never ceased, but sometimes prefixes are adopted with no clear meaning and everyone uses them according to his/her own understanding (Nomikou, 2015).

Yet certain terms become so trendy at some point that they can be considered distinctive watchwords of that historical time. This was the case of the epithet 'new', a favourite slogan for modernity propagandists who generalised it in all media, from advertising to university handbooks. It is not surprising that museum scholars hailed then the label 'new museology', which was coined with broad success in French, albeit some rare precedents of this expression had been documented in other languages. After the revolution of May 1968 in Paris, the *nouveau roman*, the *nouvelle histoire*, the *nouvelle vague* or other similar designations became ubiquitous in the Francophone world. It was in that very context where the label *nouvelle muséologie* also emerged to identify a museological break, whose charismatic leader was George-Henri Rivière, seconded by a devoted circle of close compatriots, such as Hugues de Varine-Bohan, Matilde Bellaigue and André Desvallées, but also by many followers from other countries, notably in Canada, where the *Mouvement Internationale pour une Nouvelle Muséologie* (MINOM) originated as the outcome of a cross-continental workshop on ecomuseums held in Quebec in 1984. There one leading figure was Pierre Mayrand, the great apostle who thereafter expanded the new-museological faith by making disciples in not only French-speaking nations but also in other cultural areas.[2] Such was their success that this label has been later adopted in all languages, although it is often incorrectly used to refer to recent trends in museum studies, which may be new but should no longer be called 'new museology'.

The French expression *nouvelle muséologie* conveys a situated historic meaning which, as is the case with so many terminological categorisations, can easily be lost in translation.[3] A comparable example would be the coetaneous English appellation 'New Art History', specifically used by a progressive faction of art historians who flourished since the 1970s.[4] Born at the same time, the expression *nouvelle muséologie* also has a given connotation that is not deductible from the literal meaning of words and has led to misunderstandings in other linguistic contexts. Warning against these confusions, the specialised glossary *Key Concepts of Museology* published in French, English and Spanish by the International Council of Museums (Desvallées & Mairesse, 2010: 55), clarifies that the 'new museology' *par excellence* was a trend that emerged in France in the 1970s, and one that has expanded internationally since 1984 with the main claim of more socially engaged museums. Most particularly, the crux of the matter was a new museum type, the ecomuseum, characterised as a triple novelty. Firstly, far from being housed in a building, its location should encompass an entire territory. Secondly, rather than conserving a collection, it would deal with a broad heritage of material and immaterial culture. Finally, above all, it had to be self-managed by the community as a whole, instead of being run by curators or other museum staff. That was the neo-museologists' favourite hobbyhorse, their great contribution and perhaps also their main limitation: although pioneering *ecomusées* raised high expectations at that time, particularly the first French foundations, the eventual survival of these establishments was fleeting and, due to their location in deep France, they barely had any influence on the main museums of the capital. All in all, the impact of ecomuseums in current cultural policies was very restricted despite their impressive international expansion.[5]

Nevertheless, their museological repercussion was immense. Although MINOM activists were fundamentally people of action, for whom theorisation was not their main goal, they had an enormous influence on academic stances as the glory days of the *nouvelle muséologie* coincided with a major flowering of museum studies worldwide. One of the countries then leading such development of publications and courses on museums was the United Kingdom, but the evangelisation of the 'new museology' that ignited there through a parallel initiative eventually resulted in a schism. The left-wing ideological profile of French *nouvelle muséologie* was very much in tune with the progressive ideas of some scholars and curators whose texts were gathered by Peter Vergo, Professor of Art History at the University of Essex, in a collective volume published in 1989 entitled *The New Museology*. However, in its pages there was no mention of MINOM, whose members felt very upset and ever more offended because that book soon became universally known and quoted and eclipsed the 'true' neo-museological church. The justified indignation of those who felt that their inspiring banner had been opportunistically snatched for an English bestselling title would, in any case, have the positive effect of provoking André Desvallées, the erstwhile assistant to Georges-Henri Rivière at the Musée National des Arts et Traditions Populaires, to edit the true neo-museological 'Bible' (Gómez Martínez, 2006: 274). Poetically titled – perhaps to pay homage to the *nouvelle vague* of French cinematography – *Vagues: Une anthologie de la nouvelle muséologie*, the first volume of this compilation, published in 1992, was like an 'Old Testament' of texts authored by revered predecessors and pioneers from the 1970s and 1960s or even earlier; the second, published in 1994, compiled texts of recent apostles – especially French, but not exclusively – which obviously included none of the authors of the 'apocryphal' new-museological gospel edited by Peter Vergo.[6] Disagreement would last for decades as many authors of the Anglosphere continued to vaguely use the expression 'new museology' after the book with that title without referring to the previous development of *nouvelle muséologie*. This continued and led to misunderstandings or problems of communication among museologists from different schools, even within ICOM, where English has become the universal lingua franca but is, inevitably, spoken and understood according to the respective cultural background.

Some reactions in favour or against 'new museology' and the following tendencies must thus be elucidated in the light of relevant national or disciplinary differences (Stam, 1993; Marstine, 2006: 5). At first glance it is easy to, for example, misread a well-known sentence by Mieke Bal that criticises new museology for being 'focused first on the ethnographic and second on the historical museum, whereas the art museum is less intensely addressed' (Bal, 1996: 202): one would be tempted to infer that she was blaming Rivière and his MINOM followers. Nevertheless, the ensuing bibliographical note refers to Peter Vergo's book, which was indeed culturally closer to the famous Dutch artist and theorist (Bal, 1996: 215, note 3). Authors with a very broad reading range in linguistic terms attempted to keep an equanimous distance between ensuing museological waves by combining measured words of sympathy or disaffection. The demand to confer people and not only officialdom, greater representation, referred to a long tradition of progressive changes in which both 'new museology' and 'critical museology' should be considered akin according to Marjorie Halpin, curator of the Museum of Anthropology at the University of British Columbia (Halpin, 1997). Michael M. Ames, the charismatic director of that museum between 1974 and 1997, was at that time identified with new museology's commitment to empower the community (Ames, 1990); yet he later qualified this support by arguing that professional curators should ultimately be in charge of museum interpretation, and he critically warned about the risks of 'adulterated museology' or 'counterfeit museology' (Ames, 2006). An equally balanced perspective would be that of Peter van Mensch, director of the MA in Museology at the Reinwardt Academy in Amsterdam and Leiden from 1987 until he retired in 2011. In many ways, his research and teaching served as a cross-cultural bridge between opposing poles: he took a doctorate in Museology at Zagreb University,[7] thus becoming one of the few connectors between pioneering Central European museologists and the 'new museology' rebels. He thereafter cultivated a diplomatic attitude, which he perhaps acquired between 1989 and 1993 during his presidency of ICOM's International Committee for Museology (ICO-FOM), when he would repeatedly show great mental openness as to other currents, specifically regarding 'critical museology'. Van Mensch mentions it in many of his texts, often as the second element of a joint binomial: 'new museology and critical museology'. For him they are never separate either conceptually or chronologically because, according to his personal recollections, the name 'critical museology' was already used back in the 1970s by Reinwardt Academie students, albeit circumstantially and without the meaning that this expression would later attain.[8]

This precedent was mentioned in 1983 by Lynne Teather in her monumental doctoral dissertation *Museology and Its Traditions*, a title that appropriately conveys her global vision of the evolution of museum studies as a historical continuum of accumulative contributions (Teather, 1984: 27). Then she went back to Canada, at the University of Toronto, where she suggested varied adjectives for museology, such as 'reflective' or 'reflexive' (Teather, 1991), 'transformative' or 'transformational' (Teather, 2009) but, above all, 'critical' (Teather & Carter, 2009) until a combination emerged: 'critical reflexive' (Teather, 2012). Many of her favourite intellectual referents were postmodern museologists, such as Susan Pearce, Eileen Hooper-Greenhill or Tony Bennett, although none had ever expressly identified himself or herself with 'critical museology' or its name variants, adopted by Teather as a transposition from the 'critical pedagogy' championed by revered education specialists such as Henry Giroux or Roger Simon. Following their footsteps, other adherents mushroomed in different cultural areas, as evidenced in Spanish by the early publication of books with the title *museología crítica*, both by university professors of heritage education and museum staff involved in pedagogical work (Lorente & Almazán, 2003; Santacana & Hernández Cardona, 2006; Rodrigo, 2007) (Figure 1.2). Prof. Teather in the meantime stepped back from that battle of names when she became president of ICOM's International Committee for the Training of Personnel (ICTOP) between 2008 and 2016, a period during which she carefully avoided being identified with any sectarian label. Yet others have taken over and 'critical pedagogy' continues to be a major disciplinary basis for 'critical museology', which has been especially developed and has not emerged by coincidence in either museum departments of education and public outreach or university courses of museum education.

Social thinkers are, however, often referred to as the main theoretical inspiration for critical museologists, whose doctrinal principles were reportedly firstly inspired by the theories of Theodor Adorno and Max Horkheimer (according to Poulot, 2005: 105; Navarro Rojas, 2006; Navarro & Tsagaraki, 2009/10 2009). Drawing on Derrida and Foucault or other postmodern philosophers, a new breed of influential publications on museums preferred to place emphasis on discrepancies and breakpoints (Mason, 2006; Karp et al., 2006). Thereafter, Bruno Latour's epistemological cogitations on science and society have also had substantial influence (Mairesse, 2015). Yet in terms of ideas or ideology, there has been no definite watershed singling out of critical museologists from previous museum theorists; the growing influence of feminism and gender studies at the turn of the millennium could not be understood without contemplating the pioneering contributions of previous generations in both museology and other knowledge areas. The name 'critical sociology' existed in England before the treatises of Anthony Giddens, Stuart Hall, Paul DuGay, Mike Featherstone, etc. Postmodernism brought along a nominal transformation of many disciplines that defiantly

Figure 1.2 Book covers of two pioneering volumes on critical museology in Spanish.

declared a 'critical' turn; but for many years all we got was a catchy label with no specific meaning. Everyone understood 'critical museology' differently, and many scholars would soon suggest variations or alternative designations.

'Reflexive museology' could have been a much better choice, as Ruth Phillips accurately suggested, if the main point was to vindicate an intellectual discourse, a thinking engagement (Phillips, 2003). Indeed in the new millennium, reflexivity seems to have become the holy mantra that is enthusiastically proclaimed by all (Macdonald & Basu, 2007: 20). Yet it is well-known that to reflect means both thinking and mirroring, a postmodern conundrum much talked about in all disciplines that has also inspired frequent deliberations about the adjectives 'reflective' or 'reflexive' in museology (Teather, 1991; Butler, 2013; Brulon Soares, 2015; Davidson, 2015; Pagani, 2017; Message, 2018: 74). 'Representational' could have similar meanings with closer bonds to 'representation', another sacred key word in social sciences, which gave rise to the composite designation 'representational critique', used in the introduction to a monumental museological compilation (Macdonald, 2006: 3). How to (re)present contentious issues, opposing views and museological controversies in museums would be the axis of critical museology from the point of view of communication sciences (Hasian & Wood, 2010). Drawing on the dual interpretation of 'representation' by cultural theorist Stuart Hall, museologist Óscar Navarro argued that critical museology is all about dynamics of symbolic power by taking into account museums as markers of our collective ethical perceptions and considering how they reflect our society (Navarro, 2012: 29). Therefore, if matters of social inclusion in museums also define the key issues of critical museology, then it is not so ultimately different from 'new museology', which in its last reformulation has in fact become known as 'socio-museology'. Their differences are often very nuanced in the eyes of certain Latin American theoreticians more prone to pragmatic syncretism (Morales Moreno, 2015, 2019; Aidar, 2020). Actually, community museums and their museological supporters continue to flourish in Mexico more than anywhere in the world, unencumbered by the huge success reached there by the expression *museología crítica* in academic circles but also in official political initiatives or in joint ventures, such as the 'William Bullock Chair of Critical Museology' created in 2015 by the National Autonomous University of Mexico (UNAM), together with the National Institute of Fine Arts (INBA) and the British Council.

Attaining officialdom might seem paradoxical for critical museology, or for any other discipline with that designation. It is true enough that to be critical is primarily understood as being against by expressing contestation. That has certainly been a common feature of socially engaged museologists, always eager to stand up for those on the fringes of society (Hernández, 2018: 135). Contesting race and gender discrimination became a top priority among English-speaking museologists as a consequence of the 'culture wars' in the United States of America and Canada, which then extended to Australia, New Zealand, or to other countries with indigenous minorities or multicultural citizenship who have a claim to a fair treatment in hegemonic culture and whose institutions should reflect a society with plural identities (Cameron, 1995; MacDonald & Fyfe, 1996; Simpson, 1996). Indeed even in French-speaking museology, which previously centred on ecomuseums and territorial *musées de société* driven by grassroots collectives, the focus was moving to contentious cultural representation in museums and collections with a more heterogeneous vision vis à vis heritage and citizenship. Then the most talked-about case was the Musée d'Ethnographie in Neuchâtel, pioneering postmodern critical irony and the deconstruction of speeches about 'the others' (Beuvier, 2003; Gonseth, 2013; Van Geert, 2018: 287). Similarly in Spanish-speaking countries, interest turned from the participation and empowerment of indigenous communities in rural areas to more ideologically driven institutions, epitomised in, for example, Chile by the Museum of Memory and Human Rights by eclipsing attention from the Mapuche Museum, which had been the main legacy of Chilean 'new museology' according to Luis Alegría, who identifies 'critical museology' in his country with the return to democracy and promoting plurality of interpretations (Alegría Licuime, 2013: 8). Later, the Jewish Museum in Warsaw was presented as the quintessence of critical museologies in post-communist Poland (Kirshenblatt-Gimblett, 2015). Meanwhile, the fervent defence of 'otherness' brought a moment of crisis for both ethnology and ethnological museums, still identified with familiar samples of regional folklore and other elements of home-grown traditions, which were culturally close in time and space terms (Kirshenblatt-Gimblett, 1991; Roigé, 2007; Grinell & Gustavsson Renius, 2013). Conversely, with a more universal and heterogeneous vision, both of heritage and citizenship, global prestige was on the rise for anthropology (a more recent discipline with a greater critical distance regarding its subject of study, according to Marcus & Fischer, 1986). Instead of traditional rural heritage with nationalist overtones and nostalgic 'ethnomelancholy' (Grau Lobo, 2020: 159), transnational issues regarding multicultural relations would lie in the eye of the hurricane, such as the restitution of colonial collections or the relativity of treasured values, which became the favourite subject for anthropologists who define themselves as 'critical' (Smith, 2012; Winter, 2012; Witcomb & Buckley, 2013: 573; Bodenstein & Pagani, 2014). Their influence on museum work would lead to a disciplinary deviation from usual ethnology displays towards the typical standard staging practices of art galleries to enhance the aesthetic qualities of pieces of material culture (Celis, 2017). Large museums in the capitals of former colonial empires then changed their configuration, and even their name, from ethnology to anthropology (Pagani, 2017: 76–77). It was in this context when the Madrid institution that between 1940 and 1993 had been called National Museum of Ethnology recovered its former name of National Museum of Anthropology and, not by chance, has been reformulated at the turn of the millennium in the light of critical theories. Nor is coincidental the name 'Laboratory of Experimental Audiovisual Anthropology' given to the workshop of critical practices on relational identity in one of the Spanish institutions most identified with critical museology, the Museo de Arte Contemporáneo (MUSAC) in León (Flórez Crespo, 2006; Sola, 2014): to the point that the visit starts in Room 1, an educational-relational space for (self-)reflection that aims to showcase the crisis in the arts system.

1.2 Further transdisciplinary interinfluences: the way towards 'critical heritology'

Thus, a pivotal disciplinary turn to be taken into account for its direct impact on 'critical museology' could be the triumph of 'critical anthropology', with outstanding authors like Ivan Karp and Steven Lavine in the USA, Shelley Ruth Butler in Canada or British-born expatriates Mary Bouquet and Anthony Alan Shelton. The latter has indeed been one of the most enthusiastic champions of 'critical museology' throughout his professional life as a museum curator – he was the director of the Horniman Museum in London when he founded the editorial series 'Contributions in Critical Museology and Material Culture' – and all along his brilliant academic career, first at the University of Sussex, where he created a master's degree in Critical Museology, then in Coimbra (Portugal), and at the University of British Columbia (Canada) since 2004, where he has directed the Museum of Anthropology until June 2021. Therefore, he is deservedly considered a high authority as both a museum professional and a museum scholar who spans the fields of art and anthropology (Shelton, 2001). Yet he has remained most faithful mainly to anthropological studies as regards his research subjects, the bibliography he quotes (or does not) and the predecessors he pays tribute to, such as Michael Ames, James Clifford, Shelley Ruth Butler or Jacques Hainard. At MoA, his team includes declared 'critical museologists', such as Carol E. Mayer or Nuno Porto, but none is so inclined to museum theories. In this context, Professor Shelton stands out individually for his epistemological speculations, which have developed a very personal classification of museology, within which he distinguishes three categories: 'operational', 'praxiological' and 'critical' (Shelton, 2013). Such taxonomies correspond to three levels between praxis and theory that should advance as a joint line, as argued in the lengthy interview in which he paid tribute to the long path already trodden in Canadian museums regarding public representation.[9]

A nodal point in this story, Canada, defines itself as a 'multicultural' country, the paradigm of a plural approach to diversity, which is also manifested in its museums and museologists. Professor Shelley Ruth Butler, for one, has visibly identified with such political commitment since 1999, when the Royal Ontario Museum published her famous book *Contested Representations*; although her scepticism about improvements in multicultural representation and participation in museums soon leaked out in a controversial article where she asked for more critical museological discourses (Butler, 2000: 77). Despite her warnings, the infatuation with community self-management so typical of new museology has often produced museums specialised in a certain cultural minority. There is no shortage of examples in Canada, and there are even more in the United States: the Jewish Museum, the Museo del Barrio or the Italian-American Museum are three famous cases in New York, followed by the Indian-American and African-American Museum in Washington, the Arab-American in Deaborn, the countless African-American or Chinese-American museums in so many other cities and a long etcetera. These hyphenated museums are laudable initiatives, although their proliferation might be indicative of very compartmentalised citizenship not integrated into a common identity (Conn, 2010: 225; see also Holo, 2019). The final result could be a mosaic of cultures presented in the respective museum-ghetto while great generalist museums continue to ignore claims for an appropriate representation of these minorities. Multiculturalism has more to do with crossed gazes by comparatively showing how some people are perceived from the point of view of others and *vice versa* (Brown, 2004; Pieterse, 2005). This justified the dual qualification 'critical and comparative museology' used by some anthropologists (Kreps, 2006: 458).

Diversity is the key word, or 'multiversity' according to the appellation given to the research galleries that display all kinds of treasures from the permanent collection in the Museum of Anthropology at the University of British Columbia. That museum epitomises now critical museology in its discourses, even outdoors, as its main entrance is flanked by two welcoming sculptures commissioned from Musqueam artists while the public area at the rear also boasts totems and other pieces by sculptors of Haida, Gitxsan, Nisga'a or Oweekeno origin. Likewise, the collection of sculptures installed since 2004 in front of the Musée des Beaux-Arts de Montreal attempts to reflect multiculturalism with its evident diversity of styles, materials and iconography; the same as the collection in public spaces around the National Gallery of Canada in Ottawa, which includes the menhir entitled *Black Nest*, the work of Bill Vazan, whose ornamentation pays tribute to indigenous traditions. These examples that confer visibility in public spaces to a variety of vernacular cultures could remind the single *mât* – pole in French – often typically erected as a solitary totem to mark the symbolic centre in an ecomuseum (Sánchez, 2020). Yet the number makes a difference in many ways.

Neo-museologists succumbed to romantic notions of 'community' in the singular (Barrett, 2011: 111). Critical museologists should instead emphasise a plural criss-crossing of perceptions by diverse communities (Barrett, 2015: 93). In this quest, an academic expression has become providential: 'contact zones'. That concept, originally coined by linguist Mary Louise Pratt, was transferred to museum studies by anthropologist James Clifford in his famous essay 'Museums as Contact Zones', where he praised some cases of both intercultural friction and dialogue (Clifford, 1997). Subsequently, further socio-political interpretations of 'contact zones' have been made about the public representation of multiculturality within the museum studies framework (Schorch, 2013; Message, 2015: 262–265). A key issue, however, remains paramount for this representational inquiry: the display of museum collections out in the public realm. The Portland Art Museum in Oregon was the first example cited by Clifford in his article to exalt the institution's commitment to amalgamate different worldviews; later this ideal seems to have been pursued there by displaying emblematic pieces outdoors so as to convey an image of plurality. Anthropologically conscious works of contemporary art have also been conferred much visibility outdoors by a number of museums across the United States of America and all over the world (Lorente, 2019: 194–195). One of my favourite examples is the Vancouver Art Gallery, whose main entrance had already been decorated, specifically at the bottom of the stairs, with the monument entitled *Bird of Spring*, a traditional work of Eskimo artist Abraham Etungat. However, since 2001, its roof is crowned by a conceptual installation of the eminent Chinese-Canadian artist Ken Lun, who had a different ship placed in every corner of the building, and each oriented to one of the cardinal points and painted in red, yellow, black and white, the respective stereotypical colours of the Indian, Asian, African and Caucasian races. Hence its eloquent title *Four Boats Stranded: Red and Yellow, Black and White* (Lorente, 2011). Another even more remarkable case is the National Art Gallery of Pakistan, opened in 2007 in the political epicentre of Islamabad, next to the Parliament and the presidential mansion. Outside its main door it presents, with the appropriate museum label, the sculpture *Seven Feelings against Destruction* by world-famous artist Rabia Zuberi, a woman and immigrant from India, the rival country in many concerns: thus the museum seems to publicly reaffirm itself as 'a place of reflection rather than nationalistic assertion' (Knell, 2016: 114–115). Prof. Erica T. Lehrer, who is one of the promoters of critical museology studies at Concordia University in Montreal and a great expert on memory of Jewish heritage in Poland, has also offered further examples of museums and public art policies of identity and reconciliation (Lehrer, 2016). It is a sign of development of any society that its minorities are not only tolerated but are also visibly present in the public sphere and, therefore, museums are also required to assume that righteous claim.

So now more than ever, the promotion of positive values of equality, tolerance and democratic culture should be considered a priority goal for museologists. Once again, this is a long-term struggle with changing strategies in different historical periods. An optimistic fervour of progress was usually identified with modernity and also with MINOM declarations fervently proclaimed by standing adepts at the end of their meetings. But it would be an exaggeration to fall now on the opposite pole. The word 'criticism' is not necessarily synonymous with invective or negative opinion but rather with judgemental appreciation or assessment. This has always been the basis for the work of art critics and art historians. It is no surprise that the arts sector has been particularly prolific in critical studies of museums. In fact, the expression 'critical museology' had been used earlier by some art experts who wrote in Spanish and French.[10] Yet the most influential essays by critical art historians and museologists came to be published in English, particularly in the United States of America. A prominent forerunner in this field was Carol Duncan, a Professor of Art History at Ramapo College in New Jersey: In 1993 she published *The Aesthetics of Power: Essays in Critical Art History*, followed two years later by her best-known book *Civilizing Rituals Inside Public Art Museums*, a milestone in political/feminist criticism of art gallery displays (Duncan, 1995). Professor Jo-Anne Berelowitz soon seconded her on the West Coast and many others all over the world; most were members of an age group marked by Marxist and materialist studies, plus other elements of a fertile ground that nurtured their critical analysis of culture, as acknowledged by Daniel J. Sherman and Irit Rogoff in the presentation of a volume based on conference papers (Sherman & Rogoff, 1994: xiii). This inspired my naive interpretation of succeeding museological trends in terms of a battle of generations, when I defiantly proclaimed 'New museology is dead, long live critical museology!' in the title of the introduction to another collective book (Lorente & Almazán, 2003: 13–25).

More accurate was my impression that our militancy should be especially strong in the contemporary art field. The art system had been challenged for decades by artists and curators, then followed by innumerable academics, whose critical reassessments of art institutions deployed scholarly evaluations of their collections, architecture, social role and political history in light of the latest cultural theories. On the Los Angeles campus of the University of California, Prof. Donald Preziosi became a referential figure for postmodern criticism in art history and museology or, as he preferred to say, 'critical museum studies' (Preziosi & Farago, 2004: 475). This circumlocution was added to the complicated disparity of names and denominations in both English and other languages, in which neologisms such as anti-museum, post-museum or other utopian terms were considered. The result was an intricate forest of concepts in which one could too easily get lost, according to Petra Hanáková, a professor at the Academy of Performing Arts in Bratislava. In her long article in Slovak, based on her doctoral thesis, she pessimistically pointed out the difficulties of defining *kritickej muzeológie* and the rather scarce real impact of so much verbiage on art museums around the world (Hanáková, 2005; cf. also Orišková, 2006).

Meanwhile, another appeal to more critical positions within institutions was made by performer artist and essayist Andrea Fraser using a witty wordplay 'From the Critique of Institutions to an Institution of Critique' as the title of her famous article published in *Artforum* (Fraser, 2005). Then David Carrier, philosopher and prolific author of essays on art history, provocatively titled *Museum Skepticism* a remarkable book, which began with the claim that the same freedom enjoyed by professors to express themselves critically should be exercised by their colleagues in museums (Carrier, 2006: x). Of course, the eco of judgemental academic discourses was resonating in museums and, as Andrea Fraser acknowledged, most particularly in those devoted to contemporary art, whose educators, curators, directors and architects have always been very much aware of such criticism, but they would most often respond silently through their practice rather than joining their voices in a polyphony of opinions.

Could institutions in fact be critical? Would museums be able to criticise and become the subject and not just the object of such a verb? Some authors believed so and, to paraphrase Fraser, the ideal of a critical museum seemed a reality at hand's reach (Chiodi, 2009; Zuliani, 2009; Piotrowski, 2011). There were even those who optimistically proclaimed the imminent advent of a 'radical museum' which would cultivate democracy, dialogue and debate (Chamberlain, 2011). *Radical Museology* was, thus, the name given to this institutional activism by Claire Bishop, a Professor of Art History at the City University of New York and the author of an excellent book that tracks good examples of controversial initiatives across museums of contemporary art (Bishop, 2013). A coetaneous volume with another emphatic title *Postcritical Museology: Theory and Practice in the Art Museum* declared that the time had come for the Tate Gallery and other art museums to adopt educational policies of democracy, inclusion and multiculturalism beyond mere academic discourses identified with critical museology, of which the three editors of the book had just enough (Dewdney, Dibosa & Walsh, 2013). Some of them were university lecturers, which coloured their demands for a greater interrelation of museological theory with empirical work, a claim subsequently reinforced by Victoria Walsh in her paper for a collective volume whose title *From Museum Critique to the Critical Museum* seemed to also insist on that crucial correlation: indeed the contents reviewed all sorts of challenging developments in art museums from the nineteenth century onwards, with a special focus placed on post-communist European countries (Murawska-Muthesius & Piotrowski, 2015) (Figure 1.3).

Therefore, notwithstanding the persistent fascination for 'institutional critique' in the art world, alternative nomenclatures have flourished by advocating more proactive approaches (Leshchenko, 2009). Most importantly, a broader mindframe has made its way beyond art and museums. Art historians, archaeologists and other cultural experts have been joining forces since 2011 at the Critical Heritage Studies Association to promote social engagement by placing a special emphasis on human rights, post-colonial perspectives, questions of self-representation, institutional narratives, etc. (Harrison, 2013) 'Critique' or 'critical' are still favourite terms, yet museum studies are losing centrality in recent bibliographical production and increasingly also turn to public art, historic monuments and other cultural legacies. In our times of rampant interdisciplinarity, the most successful label is Heritage Studies or its equivalents in other languages, particularly in Eastern Europe, where it seems that they have been talking about 'heritology' for many years while it is still rare to find any mention of critical museology there (Ananiev, 2013). In this way, the current trend towards cultural syncretism also marks a return to the founding fathers of museology: Stránský considered museal entities to be all sorts of products both inside and outside museums. In the same way, if the new museology consecrated the notion of intangible heritage, it is also of central importance for 'critical heritologists', who consider that something is defined as heritage not because of its physical qualities but for its emotional value and, thus, ultimately all heritage is intangible (Smith, 2012: 17). Laurajane Smith's critical puzzle is joining a growing tendency towards intellectual transpositions and interconnections beyond differences.

Perhaps, a more positive re-appreciation of our predecessors is actually a defining feature of critical heritage studies, which is 'looking back in order to look forward', as suggested by the beautiful title of an article commending constructive dialogue between museum practitioners and external heritage experts (Witcomb & Buckley, 2013: 573). New museology, scarcely

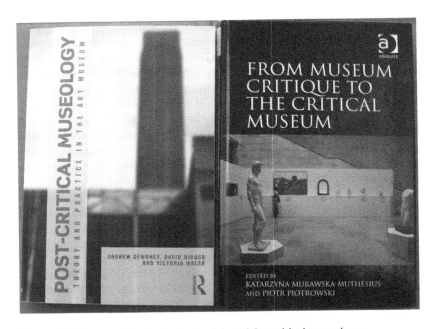

Figure 1.3 Covers of two books in English revising critical museology.

concerned about the origins of our discipline, insisted on preaching a fresh new start, but critical museologists tend to historically reconsider past and present disciplinary developments, as exemplified by the books published by the research group *Museología Crítica y Estudios de Patrimonio Cultural* at the National University of Colombia (e.g. Combariza, López Rosas & Castell, 2014). Highlighting this nominal link of 'critical museology' with heritage in Bogotá becomes important here to prove that it is not just a fashionable English expression imported from contemporary art jargon as it is travelling back and forth between diverse heritage scholars and languages (Mairesse, 2015). There are reasons for optimism, despite Jan Dolák's scathing 'critique of critical museology' (Dolák, 2016) because it is now a recurrent concept in a variety of languages and disciplines (Guzin-Lukic, 2017: 119; Semedo & Ferreira, 2017: 101; Noronha, 2017: 65–75; Ayala Aizpuro & Cuenca-Amigo, 2019). Such cultural migration has been pointed out by Prof. Bruno Brulon at the Federal University of Rio de Janeiro State in an eloquent paper appealing for a post-colonial reconsideration of museum studies by linking the contributions of museologists from different cultures (Brulon Soares, 2018: 68). An excellent materialisation of such universalist approach is a collective book, conceived from this transdisciplinary and intercultural perspective, published by the Museum of Contemporary Art of the National Autonomous University of Mexico (Figure 1.1), in whose pages Professor Luis Gerardo Morales, after advocating for the end of the separation between theory and praxis or between heritage inside and outside the museum, identified 'critical museology' with a reflective stance on the forms of communication and interpretation practices, not only of museums and exhibitions but of the expanded 'museal' field in a broad sense (Morales Moreno, 2019: 213). It is a perfect closing remark for this historical outline of some cultural contexts and disciplines in which the expression 'critical museology' has been bouncing, and gaining strength along the way, like a snowball.

Notes

1 None of these nomenclatures has become customary, although the term 'museality', coined by Stránský to refer to museum quintessence beyond the contingencies of museums, has become so influential that today he is considered one of the pioneers of 'metamuseology'; that is, theoretical reflections not centred on museums but on museology itself (Hernández, 2006: 55–58; te Heesen, 2012: 161; Brulon Soares, 2017: 156).

2 All international committees and organisations affiliated to ICOM are named using the acronyms corresponding to the initials of their designation in English, except for MINOM, founded in 1985. The prevalent language in their meetings and publications has always been French, but in recent years, much of the neo-museological bibliography is also expressed in Portuguese as some universities in both Brazil and Portugal have become strongholds of new museology and its derivations, like 'socio-museology', a term fostered by Mário Moutinho, a professor at the Universidade Lusófona of Lisbon.

3 Therefore, to avoid confusion, it may be better to always say *nouvelle muséologie*, and maintain the French nomenclature, in the same way when we avoid translating the expression *art nouveau*, which no longer refers to the newest in art as it specifically designates a particular cultural movement that flourished around 1900: the equivalent terms in other languages are quite equivocal.

4 Those progressive art historians claiming for a social and popular bias had a long-standing impact on other related disciplines, such as anthropology or history (Message, 2018: 60 note 15). Ultimately, however, the New Art History founded by T. J. Clark in the 1970s, then proudly invoked by A. L. Rees and Frances Borzello in the title of a famous 1986 book, has become a subject of historiography, which refers to it in a past tense (Harris, 2001).

5 Much has been written about the internationalisation of ecomuseums, especially in Francophone countries like Nigeria or Canada, or in Latin America, where it converged with the 'community museums' promoted in Mexico by the National Institute of Anthropology and History. A broad global overview of this new-museological development, which summarised the copious existing bibliography, has been offered by excellent books in English (Davis, 1999), French (De Varine, 2017) or Spanish (Navajas, 2020).

6 Unfortunately, the promoters in turn incurred in a similar cultural chauvinism, because despite the fact that MINOM recruited a good part of its militancy in Latin America, there were no texts by Spanish-speaking or Portuguese-speaking museologists in *Vagues* (Desvallées, 1992 &1993).

7 His doctoral thesis (Mensch, 1992) can be downloaded freely at http://emuzeum. cz/admin/files/Peter-van-Mensch-disertace.pdf (it has also been published in French by ICOFOM in L'Harmattan). From it, the author produced many other publications on the subject of museum studies and training (notably Mensch, 1990, 1992, 1996, Mensch & Meijer-Van Mensch, 2015). A related conciliatory figure would be Ivo Maroević, a Professor at the University of Zagreb, who after a period of years at the University of Victoria (Canada) made interesting connections with critical museology (Maroević 1998).

8 Apparently around 1979, an unnamed lecturer started to instigate students to write an assessment of museums visited on their own, mixed with the rest of the public, to develop personal criticism, unbiased by the museum staff explanations received during scheduled school visits. This was sardonically dubbed 'critical museology' at the Reinwardt Academie, but not even there would that label ever reach serious echoes afterwards.

9 Answering a question from Gustaaf Houtman on how he would characterise his international career in the world of museums, Shelton declared: 'Above all I want to contribute to a reorganization and critical appreciation of museums and material and visual cultures in our lives as a necessary pre-condition for engendering new forms and subjects of and for public representation' (Houtmann, 2009: 8).

10 An essay about museum architecture first published in 1992 by French curator Maurice Besset included, with no precise meaning, the expression 'critical museology', which had also been haphazardly used a decade before by Argentine curator and art critic Jorge Glusberg when explaining his concept of 'cold' museums (Lorente, 2012: 249, footnote 23).

2 Museums in question, self-questioning museums

Figure 2.1 Self-reflexive display about what it is (not) usually shown at the National Archaeological Museum, Athens.

DOI: 10.4324/9781003263050-3

2.1   From 'institutional critique' to 'critical institutionalism'

Artists have always been the foremost and keenest critics of museums. From the Enlightenment period onwards some of the most severe comments on museums, academies and other art institutions have come from them. Such invectives, however, would turn particularly spiteful in the case of the Futurists and other early twentieth-century avant-garde groups. Another historical landmark was set in January 1969 when Takis removed his kinetic sculpture from a show in the MoMA. He demanded his right to decide if and how his artwork should be displayed – even though it was the museum's property. His protest was backed by Sol Lewitt and others who also claimed that a fee be paid to artists by collectors of their artworks. Subsequently, in the 1970s champions of Conceptual art such as Marcel Broodthaers, Daniel Buren, Michael Asher, Hans Haacke and Isidoro Valcárcel instituted as a new art genre the creation of artworks that confront the authority of the temples of culture. Their challenging artistic indictments came to be referred to as 'institutional critique', a special trend soon deeply rooted within the institutional system of art. Scholars often stress this paradox, pointing out that many artists from recent generations have carved their careers and fame out of their attacks on museums or the art system while those very museums and exhibition centres commissioned them and then published catalogues, monographs or critical essays of their work.[1] As a matter of fact, the growing bibliography on this art genre is already quite extensive, with books about internationally acclaimed figures including Fred Wilson, Alfredo Jaar, Mark Dion or Cesare Pietroiusti (Welchman, 2006; Chiodi, 2009). Furthermore, in the wake of artists such as Louise Lawler – renowned for her puzzling displays of prestigious artworks and collections – some artists have specialised in a subgenre of 'institutional critique' creating a peculiar professional category: the artist-curator, that is the artist supplanting the curator (Zuliani, 2009: 59–83). An issue worth examining.

In museum studies literature, a milestone was marked by the *succès de scandale* caused by the caustic 1992 touring exhibition *Mining the Museum* displayed at the Maryland Historical Society and other museums. African-American artist Fred Wilson combined products of eighteenth and nineteenth-century North American high culture with historical material recalling black slavery and drew massive academic attention worldwide (Corrin, 1994; Shelton, 2001; Bernier, 2002; Belda Navarro & Marín Torres, 2004). Usually referred to as one of the instances which paved the way for critical museology, anthropologist Peter H. Welsh, however, pointed out that some of the acclaim Wilson received ought to have been shared by the staff of the museums hosting such call on the collective conscience

(Welsh, 2005: 119). Something that perhaps has not been stressed enough is the fact that the Maryland Historical Society was already in the process of questioning its exhibition discourse and chose to commission Wilson on the occasion of the annual meeting of the American Association of Museums held in Baltimore. The museum professionals gathered there became the most enthusiastic audience of the exhibition, propitiating its extraordinary success and repercussion, as Eva-Maria Troelenberg explains (in Troelenberg & Savino, 2017: 4). Critical museologists are unquestionably indebted to artists, particularly to those subverting humdrum routines, but must we persist in the blinkered approach perceiving the artist as a stereotypical 'genius' to be extolled above all other humans?

A museum that seeks to spark critical deliberation may feel tempted to delegate such tasks to artists, as society more readily accepts unconventional and unsettling reappraisals coming from them. Many companies and institutions adopt this strategy, happy to have their image revamped, with an innovative and even rebellious tinge, thanks to the defiant creativity of artists and designers. Likewise, the interventions of some contemporary artists may have ironically served as cosmetics in providing an outwardly postmodern critical image to institutions which deep inside remain loyal to a rather traditional approach. Nonconformist art would thus be used as a shield to absorb or deflect the piercing attacks on museums, as Gaëlle Crenn claims to have been the case at the Belgian Musée Royal de l'Afrique Centrale, following the precedent set by the Parisian Musée du Quai Branly (Crenn, 2016). This critical coating is even more frequent in contemporary museums and art centres, usually surrounded by artworks of 'institutional critique' visibly displayed in adjacent public areas to grant them a glamorously rebellious touch which virtually acts as a preventive attack. The Conceptual artworks set in Seville at the Centro Andaluz de Arte Contemporáneo and in Madrid at the entrance to the Museo Nacional Centro de Arte Reina Sofía in the square created after the extension by Jean Nouvel in 2005 constitute highly eloquent instances of this phenomenon. Rogelio López Cuenca, one of Spain's leading artists in the genre of 'institutional critique', had been commissioned to create a piece for the Universal Exposition of Seville in 1992. He set up 23 information panels resembling the official ones but holding inextricable and sarcastic messages. Concerned with the possibility that visitors could be misled, the authorities had them removed on the eve of the inauguration of the World Fair. Most of them were donated to the Centro Andaluz de Arte Contemporáneo (CAAC) and some were sent to Museo Nacional Centro de Arte Reina Sofía (MNCARS). Both institutions have them displayed outside their premises and both have appropriately placed in the doorway, the pieces rephrasing, on both sides, the signpost that Dante envisaged welcoming those who arrive in Hell: *Lasciate ogni speranza, voi ch'entrate.* (Divine Comedy, Canto III).

LASCIAT/EOGNISP/Eranzas/Pettatoriq/Uestoéun/Oespettacolo
LEAVE/ALLHOP/Espect/Ators/Thisisa/Spectacle

VERLAβT/JEDE/Hoffnung/Zuschauer/Das iste/Ine Schau
LAISSEZ/TOUTES/Poirsp/Ectaeurs/Ceciestu/NSpectacle

Imagine the reactions of the visitors at the CAAC or the MNCARS who are patient and knowledgeable enough to decipher the intricate texts conveying López de Cuenca's sardonic message: 'Leave all hope spectators: this is a spectacle' (Figure 2.2). Funnily enough, he meant the 1992 Universal Exposition, yet his warning perfectly suits the entrance to these two centres of cultural 'spectacles', the greatest flagships of their respective arts districts in Seville and Madrid (Lorente, 2019: 176). As a matter of fact, other museums also welcome visitors with an equally perturbing message, for example, the neon sign of visual poet Julien Blaine at the entrance to the Musée d'Art Contemporain of Marseille, warning visitors: *Il est encore temps de rebrousser nimehc* (you still have time to retrace your way – the last word written backwards). However, this example does flaunt a museum label, as do all the artworks in the collection of the CAAC and of the MNCARS set in public spaces, save for these pieces by Rogelio López Cuenca at his own request. He must find this appropriate as they were devised to be mistaken for official panels, expecting to baffle viewers and spark perplexity and reflection in their minds. But in fact they generally go unnoticed, precisely because of the lack of a label or QR code that would refer viewers to the profuse information available on the respective museum websites.[2] A visible panel identifying this art installation should be displayed in both institutions so that museum visitors could be well aware and informed.

'Institutional critique' does have its flaws even in the case of such admirable artists as Rogelio López Cuenca and of such leading institutions as the CAAC in Seville – where every year a critical argument is put forward around which all the exhibitions and activities revolve – or in the case of Madrid's MNCARS – which has become one of the top instances of the impact of critical thinking on art institutions. Already some years ago its director, Manuel Borja-Villel, wondered whether museums could be critical and, rewording the famous paper by Andrea Fraser in *Artforum* (2005), defended a leap from criticising institutions to 'critical institutionalism' (Borja-Villel, 2010). He perhaps envisaged it as a gradual strategy whereby more relevance would be given to external curators doubling as artists and

Figure 2.2 One of the works by Rogelio López Cuenca by the entrance of the
MNCARS, Madrid.

Source: Photo by J. Pedro Lorente, with kind permission from the artist

theoreticians: such as the sculptor and professor Juan Luis Moraza, who in
2010 curated the exhibition 'El retorno de lo imaginario. Realismos entre
XIX y XXI' [The Return of the Imaginary. Realisms between the 19th and
20th centuries], a personal installation and interpretation set with pieces
from the museum's collection. The most striking action that year was actually the confrontation between contemporary and Baroque art from the
post-colonial period in a touring exhibition signed by the artists and theoreticians Alice Creischer, Max Jorge Hinderer, Silvia Rivera Cusicanqui and
Andreas Siekmann, with the attractive title '*Principio Potosí*' [Potosí Prin-
ciple] which was later taken to the Haus der Kulturen der Welt in Berlin and
to the Museo Nacional de Arte and Museo Nacional de Etnografía y Folklore in La Paz. 'Critical curatorship' was the term given to these practices
by Terry Smith in praise of the MNCARS and its director (Smith, 2012).
But these enthusiastic remarks, inspired by idealistic debates concerning
the new and thriving institutionalism, would later become more restrained

in bibliography reviewing the historical phenomenon of the artist-curator (Möntmann, 2006; Rand & Kouris, 2007; Bawin, 2014; Green, 2018).

Curating can be an artistic undertaking that must be recognised and recognisable as such. Yet, the re-readings of collections rendered in creative displays by artists do not necessarily reflect the professional standards of the museums that host them. Even more so in the case of science museums, alien to the art system, as appropriately pointed out by museologist Noémie Drouguet, with ironical remarks on the pros and cons of letting artists playfully impersonate curatorial roles. Many of them would often be merely interested in visual displays and do not offer words of explanation, not even to clarify that the whole project is just an art installation, sometimes to the bewilderment of the public – for instance in the apparently serious exhibition of a fictitious hominid and its imagined discoverer curated by the artists Luc Ewen and Jean-Luc Koening at the Museum of Natural History of Luxembourg (Drouguet, 2007). Playing the part of 'mad scientists' has become the favourite challenge for the artists who are invited to frolic with the collections of some museums sometimes producing too abstruse exhibitions, not inserted within the epistemological framework of the respective institution (Raunig & Ray, 2009; Geismar, 2015: 193–194, 200–201). Even at museums and galleries specialising in contemporary art, whose audience won't feel outraged or surprised by artistic transgressions, new displays commissioned from 'artist-curators' may seem 'cryptic', also in the sense used by biologists for camouflaging species difficult to detect. Such was the case of some pioneering instances in the 1970s, when the Documenta in Kassel included interventions by Bazon Brock, an artist, critic and professor who always sought to blur the boundaries between these professions. But it was at the turn of the millennium when many other cases proliferated that need to be dealt with separately even from a terminological viewpoint, as they signalled the path towards the artistic-curatorial hybridisation of critical pedagogies, though under other labels.

One of the first steps in this direction was a symposium held in 2006 on the occasion of the exhibition *Academy* at the MuKHa of Antwerp and at the Van Abbemuseum of Eindhoven, where the artists Susan Kelly and Valeria Graziano in collaboration with educator Janna Graham created the project *The Ambulator; or What Happens When We Take Questions for a Walk?* (Graham, Graziano & Kelly, 2016). Perhaps they served as inspiration for the expression 'pedagogical curatorship', used to refer to the work of the Uruguayan artist Luis Camnitzer in 2007 for the VI Mercosur Biennial in Porto Alegre (Brazil), where he designed spaces for relaxing, reading, reflecting and conversing, enlivened by 300 mediators who had been trained to exchange questions in conversation with the artists and curators (Sadurni Rodríguez, 2014). His work was continued in the following years by the Argentinian artist Marina De Caro in the VII Biennial of 2009 and by Pablo Helguera in the VIII Biennial of 2011; but above all it has become a personal reference for many creators who are pursuing a career as 'artist-educators'. Many view this task as a new form of artistic expression, half way between collective participatory art and artistic appropriation, though consensus does not exist in this respect (Honorato, 2014).

The term 'pedagogical curatorship' may sound redundant as curatorial work is by definition educational, but this label conveys the idea that the focus of interest during the interpretation processes is not what is exhibited but the (self-)reflections raised. Some people will visit museums to worship worthy objects and admirable knowledge, yet once there, they may be haphazardly dazzled by the radiance of 'critical institutionalism'. It will be up to each individual to open his/her eyes to a new look or to briefly blink at such a blaze. As educational institutions, museums could not ignore the revolution in learning theories which prioritise dialectic exploration in the construction of knowledge and question inherited prevailing ideas (Rodrigo, 2007). Indeed, the impact of 'critical pedagogy' proved particularly strong in the education departments of art museums, where creativity, imagination and analytical capacity are explored through 'visual thinking': for example, Kiasma in Helsinki, a museum of contemporary art where all interpretative texts accompanying art works in their exhibitions are written in this manner by members of the educational department (Tali, 2018: 142). The interpretation of visual culture thus becomes a tool for maintaining and expressing ideas in order to enhance independent assessment. Provocative and sarcastic comments suggest fresh readings of the exhibits, raising questions and uncertainties and potentially triggering audacious analysis although Irit Rogoff, in a celebrated text-manifesto regarding this educational turn, already expressed her fears that the trend would eventually become an innocuous formula (Rogoff, 2008). That is the fate of subversion once institutionalised and generally accepted, even though the growing scope of this educational questioning is quite impressive, often intertwined with artists' institutional critique, as frequent collaboration exists between artists and educators or even the combination of both roles, in the wake of the precedent set by Luis Camnitzer.

The fact is that museums and exhibition centres are increasingly engaging artists for curatorial as well as educational tasks and to carry out shared collaborations in order to explore new aspects of a progressively vigorous critical reformulation. Former external criticisms would operate from within museums. Yet, perhaps this critical turmoil should not be overrated for its impact could have been very limited inside museums, as Victoria Walsh puts it: 'it was primarily generated by curators, academics and artists outside of the museum's permanent staff who came from non-collection based spaces' (in Murawska-Muthesius & Piotrowski, 2015: 200). Such critical subversion could have run the risk of falling into the hands of sham revolutionaries, an intellectual-artistic-curatorial superstructure enclosed in its own system of high clouds where the elevated rhetorical condensation of 'critical institutionalism' would have permeated turbulent tirades yet leaving most of the staff bone dry, without seeping into the core of the museum's work. According to another point of view, the critical/reflexive storm gradually soaked the whole art system, particularly some educational services in contemporary art centres, many of whom enshrined institutional self-reflection as a favourite argument of social pedagogy (Ang, 2015; Parramón, 2018). Be that as it may, the soft rain of critical thinking did percolate deeply into museums and had an audacious influence on practical museography as some pointers clearly reveal.

2.2 Keys to critical discourse: queries, hesitations and controversies

Many museums, either in temporary shows or in the displays of their permanent collections, have gradually replaced their assertive discourses with reflections that raise questions and doubts, which constitute the most significant feature of critical museology/museography. This is obviously far from new – Socratic maieutics or Cicero's rhetoric made constant use of questions as efficient tools to convey arguments. But, is it not true that ever since the crisis of modernity and its certainties, questions are a particularly ubiquitous device, even in museums? Specialists in anthropology and social history resolutely led the way in this sense. Very soon the Musée d'Ethnographie of Neuchâtel, directed by Jacques Hainard from 1980 to 2006, became renowned for its predilection for challenging topics and ironical questions, which Hainard called *muséologie de la rupture* (Hainard, 1987; Wastiau, 2002; Van Geert, 2018). Another early instance of inquisitive museographic presentation was the anthropology section situated since 1990 in Gallery 33 of the Museum of Birmingham (United Kingdom), because of its questioning of power, religion or other major issues: in fact, plenty of display cabinets boast interrogation marks both in the permanent exhibition on the ground floor and in temporary shows on the top floor.[3] 'What is Politics? What is Society? What is Religion?', all of them profound issues questioning some of the supreme values in many civilisations. It is one of Anthony Shelton's favourite instances; though, as he has pointed out, there was another precedent in the UK set a few years earlier by the Marischal Museum of the University of Aberdeen, whose curator, Charles Hunt, had gone even further by placing on the hands of two Victorian figures of Hottentots set in an old showcase a sign written in nineteenth-century calligraphy mimicking a letter dated in 1880 which asked: 'We protest at being exhibited so. Are we curiosities or human beings? Is science more important than compassion? You have cast us in a role we would not choose' (Shelton, 1992: 25).

By simply inserting such startling message on a nineteenth-century museum display, inquisitive metamuseographical criticisms are induced without destroying it or changing it in any way. This constitutes a pioneering example which encompasses in a nutshell almost every aspect that would later be contended by the theorists of critical museology and its practical application. It has definitely inspired other museums of anthropology, including the Museo Nacional de Antropología of Madrid, where identical figures of Hottentots are displayed alongside a critical discourse on the history of the institution in the room where the visit begins. It is not just about garnishing museum labels with questions, always so effective as learning tool (Litwak, 1996), but about having them question widely accepted certainties, even the institution's discourse guidelines and its *modus operandi*. Self-reflexive interrogative exhibitions about what is – or is not – shown in great national museums with overwhelming collections are now making visitors aware of questionable display judgements (Figure 2.1). Yet, this self-questioning approach caught on before in small peripheral museums, open to experimental initiatives, such as the Mutare Museum of Zimbabwe with a project called Hot Spot, carried out since 2001 in collaboration with the Malmö Museum and the Skellefteå Museum in Sweden (Mupira, 2002).

A turning point came when a provocative line of self-questioning interrogations was assumed by a great national museum like the Parisian Musée du Quai Branly, whose inaugural exhibition in 2006 welcomed visitors by displaying showcases where European and African sculptures were paired with inquisitive signs: 'Antique ou Primitif? Classique ou Premier?' They were later removed but similar (self-)analytical parallelisms have been proposed by many other institutions such as the Musée de l'Homme in Paris, reopened in 2015. All sorts of contrasts and questions problematising its inherited legacy, exemplified by new and old restored busts of people of different races, now line the route asking: 'D'où venons nous? Un être de parole? Un être de liens? Un être de pensé? Pourquoi sommes-nous les seuls à étudier notre histoire, à imaginer notre avenir, à visiter des musées? Qu'avons -nous de si différent?'. It could well be an example of the interrogative museum coveted by Ivan Karp and Corinne Kratz, based on questions with no obvious solution (Karp & Kratz, 2015: 281). Also at the Field Museum of Chicago, the old sculptures portraying ethnic types stored away in 1969 for their offensive similarity to animals were recovered in 2016 for a long-term exhibition titled *Looking at Ourselves*, which begins with two stinging questions: 'How has our thinking on race changed? Has our thinking on race changed?' (Figure 2.3).

Figure 2.3 Looking at Ourselves room at the Field Museum, Chicago.
Source: Photo by J. Pedro Lorente, with kind permission from the museum

Such questions have obviously become a common feature in the discourse of the Museum of Anthropology of the University of British Columbia when directed by Prof. Shelton; though it seems that for the sake of variety, indirect questions came to be used to attract attention towards the enigmas posed by the exhibits, chosen precisely for their challenging nature such as a group of Mexican masks some of which, we are informed, are fake. It is one of my favourite examples, highlighted in an article in which I also commented on other instances found nearby, at the Royal British Columbia Museum of Victoria (Lorente, 2011). Its anthropology section not only would puzzle visitors by displaying empty glass cases whose contents had been returned to the original native peoples but surprised everyone with a big picture of a tavern where some men, including a protestant pastor, are drinking and playing cards. The museum label stated the author of the painting, Rowland Lee, the date of its creation, 1892, and its double title, *Slim Jim* or *The Parson Takes the Pot*, further clarifying that the canvas was in the building of the Parliament of British Columbia from its opening in 1897 until the late 1970s. But my attention was caught by an additional panel bellow sharing with visitors several conjectures on how such medio-cre painting, despite its shocking theme of a vicar drinking and playing cards, ended up there, finally asking: 'Could it be that *Slim Jim* has a much deeper meaning? What do you think?'

This type of direct question is a classic device already in common use since the times of Freeman Tilden, who contended that interpretation is not instruction but provocation and recommended engaging in conversation with visitors based on tactically posed questions to encourage personal reflection. But of course, Tilden was referring to the guides in natural parks who talk to groups of people. Museum education departments also provide guided tours to encourage interpersonal debate, yet this lively exchange cannot be easily achieved with regular museum visitors without oral interpretation. Written materials tend to be more formal. It is not usual to find in any museum an array of interpretive texts structured according to a questioning storyline as systematised at the Kelvingrove Art Gallery in Glasgow since its renovation in 2006 (O'Neill, 2010: 386). Educational services are more typically conspicuous offering extra readings for reflection in resting areas inside or between exhibition galleries. The Guggenheim Bilbao, a pioneer in Spain introducing such didactic areas in each exhibition, offers in the corridors between the rooms devoted to the permanent collection photos and interpretive texts in various languages, calling since 2013 our attention with questions such as 'How do you feel when you look at this painting?', followed by their short explanation of how important it was for Rothko to exalt feelings and emotions with his colour-field paintings, or 'Which story do these paintings hide?' then revealing in five lines that Cy Townbly wanted to do a cycle of abstract expressionist paintings inspired by the cruelty, insanity, and murder of Roman emperor Commodus. Other two institutions very well-known for methodically using interrogations are the Museo Civico di Zoologia in Rome and the Science Museum in London, two leading cases of the implementation of inquisitive educational strategies (Lorente & Moolhuijsen, 2015). Desiccated animals in the Roman museum are presented to visitors through an entertaining quiz game which makes comparisons to human beings so as to propitiate reflection on current issues regarding biodiversity. In London's Science Museum the *Who am I?* gallery, inaugurated in 2010, explains the human genome through interactive applications tackling the body and personality through questions that are encapsulated in the slogan: 'What makes you smarter than a chimp? What makes you smile? What makes you, you?' The final question deals, amongst others, with gender diversity: a controversial matter where the museum educators chose to convey questions regarding sex differentiation in social terms, showing a wide range of options, including transgender persons.

But sophisticated teaching methods are not necessarily required, as just simple text panels may contain a set of questions making visitors think about changes and uncertainties both scientific and curatorial. This is done at the Pinacoteca do Estado de São Paulo through an ambitious educational programme entitled *Arte em diálogo*, whereby a critical interrelation is established between works of art themselves and between the works of art and the viewers by means of texts written in three different languages using questions and answers. The scheme has been in place since 2011 in an attempt to foster reflection and dialogue amongst visitors to their modern and contemporary art galleries. It is a praiseworthy achievement of the Núcleo de Ação Educativa to pose so many intelligent questions with accurate answers; but some of the most effective queries are left with an open question. Indeed, it could be considered didactically counterproductive to offer the answers, as they hinder our chances of thinking of other replies which might possibly contradict those provided. Perhaps it is better to point to a variety of responses as does the Museo Naval of Cartagena de Indias when presenting the figure of a sixteenth-century European gentleman asking the question 'How did the Spanish conquistadores defeat the ferocious West Indians?' and each side of the showcase provides a different answer, all of them correct. On other occasions, the questions may implicitly contain the key to solving the enigma, as they are posed as a hypothesis that seeks the audience's endorsement and collective involvement in curatorial questions. This is skilfully achieved by the Seattle Art Museum on many of its labels. My favourite is the one next to a painting titled *The Duet* painted *circa* 1629 by the Dutch artist Jan Miense Molenaer: 'Music-making was a metaphor for lovemaking, then as now. Judging from the objects and attitudes of the sitters, do you think that is the artist's intended message?' If we had overlooked the Freudian detail of the phallic symbolism attached to the flute the woman holds in her hands or the sensual curves of the stringed instrument embraced by the man, after reading the question we will definitely look at the musical duet differently. The same applies at the Museum Wallraf-Richartz of Cologne, whose galleries of eighteenth-, nineteenth- and twentieth-century art make use of abundant questioning texts. The label next to a small-sized picture painted by Johann Hasenclever in 1850, titled *Soirée*, poses a dilemma: 'Spass oder Ernst? Was denken Sie: Stimmungvolle Darstellung einer der Sängerin andächtig lauschenden Abendgesellschaft, oder doch ein vom Maler aufgespießtes bürgerliches Ritual?' [Fun or Seriousness? What do you think: an atmospheric painting of people at a soirée listening raptly to a singer, or an empty bourgeois ritual that the painter is mocking?]

A high level of speculation can be reached through such open questions, providing they are not childish quizzes whose answer is obvious or irrelevant. Following the claims by Howard Gardner and David Perkins on how intelligence operates and on the stimulation of reasoning, it might even be advisable to let visitors ask the questions themselves. Christopher White- head has aptly pointed out that anticipating the visitors' questions – which could be different from those they would have chosen – may seem patron- ising (Whitehead, 2012a: 38); conversely, reflective self-questioning can result in ingenious subversions of values, such as the interpretation of the Canadian landscape, which questions many patriotic and artistic stereotypes at the Art Gallery of Ontario in Toronto under the title 'Arcadian Land: Seized or Lost?' (Whitehead, 2012a: 120, 125). The double choice creates a subtle and ironic distance from the nationalist-loaded innuendos typical of romantic landscape paintings, though without reaching the sarcastically challenging approach of the interpretative texts on the walls of the perma- nent gallery dedicated to Danish and Nordic art from 1750 to 1900 on dis- play since 2011 at the Statens Museum for Kunst in Copenhagen, 'one of the few national galleries that encouraged its audience to laugh' according to Simon Knell, who quotes long excerpts from gallery texts which decon- struct aged patriotic mystifications using present language and ideas, prob- lematising the notions of nation and national art (Knell, 2016: 160–161). Similarly, the last gallery of Barcelona's Museu de Historia de Catalunya has a section titled 'Portrait of contemporary Catalonia, 1980–2007' with life-sized photos of well-known or unknown Catalans of various races, ages and social backgrounds under LED-lit signs asking: 'Do we enjoy the same rights? Do we have the same opportunities? Are we more satisfied?' One leaves the museum pondering on current uncertainties that seem to fracture the firm nationalist ideology shaping its historical rendition.

The fact that national museums question the epic glorification of vernac- ular culture may seem striking yet no developed country would nowadays accept the political propaganda used by totalitarian regimes or the mass indoctrination exerted in so many museums and major exhibitions which were identified by Tony Bennet as the 'Exhibitionary Complex' of the nineteenth century. Ideological evangelisation should nowadays be more subtly conveyed, as the Mexican historian and museologist Luis Gerardo Morales claims. He perceives that museums in Mexico continue to narrate the history of the nation from a patriotic viewpoint whereas they ought to explain that their national configuration was gradually forged after the war of Independence of 1810–1821, in a process that shaped collective iden- tity precisely with the help of museums and other educational institutions (Morales Moreno, 2007). In his opinion, the 'new Mexican museology' took a leap towards an innovative social paradigm with the Museo Nacional de Culturas Populares, inaugurated in 1982, and the community museums of Oaxaca created from 1986 to 1988; but they persevered in the exalta- tion of Indian, rural and local values, with no provisos. Costa Rican Óscar

Navarro Rojas argues that museums should rather reveal historical controversies. In his opinion, critical museology ought to confront visitors with
the dilemmas of contemporary society through the eyes of history and critical memory (Navarro Rojas, 2006). There is nothing wrong with national
museums expressing their recognition of national identity/ies which continue to mould cultural idiosyncrasies worldwide, but they can also question
the lastingness of such an approach.

The same could apply to a smaller territorial scale, though political cor-
rectness seems to dictate that any local community is intrinsically praiseworthy. Years ago Peter H. Welsh, Professor of Museum Studies at the
university of Kansas, pointed out that: 'Museums are expected to be places
where the "genius of a people" is celebrated' (Welsh, 2005: 112). He gave
the extreme example of the Boston Children's Museum, for offering event
programmes specifically designed to celebrate 'your community and family'. Without going into such levels of adulation, modern society does take
it for granted that museums must approach local history and identity from
a laudatory perspective. In order to meet such expectations, visitors are
often welcomed with this type of cliché, though once inside contents are
not always quite so favourable. This is the case of the Vancouver Museum
where a welcoming sign at the entrance describes the institution's mission
as a 'celebration' of Vancouver and its history while its collection renders
indeed a bold review of the city's past, especially in the section titled *The
Gateway to the Pacific*, which narrates the changes that have taken place
since the early twentieth century contrasting the traditional view of prosperity and modernisation with poignant images of deprivation, discrimination
and racist attacks endured by Asian immigrants. This historical revisionism
is nowadays considered essential to bolster the museum's social principles,
which would be highly questionable if uncritically surrendering to propaganda at the service of a particular identity be it supranational, national,
regional, local or concerning a specific community (Gob, 2010: 153)

A notion which, by the way, ought to be assumed by the museums promoted by neo-museologists in many countries to cater for some specific
minorities. When the new building of the Canadian Museum of Civiliza-
tion was inaugurated in 1989 both the construction and its contents were
supposed to promote cultural self-esteem, therefore exclusively singing
the praises of the first nations represented there (MacDonald & Alsford,
1995: 29). It was renamed the Canadian Museum of History in 2013, but its
celebrative discourse does not seem to have changed much. The National
Museum of the American Indian in Washington DC, in the heart of an egali-
tarian democracy, has continued to place in more prominent positions the
objects belonging to persons of a higher rank in native Indian traditions
(Rosof, 2003: 74–75). Fortunately, in terms of gender equality even the

most fervent defenders of the empowering of indigenous cultures have realised that not everything about them is praiseworthy. It was not right that some tribes even demanded that women were not allowed access to objects intended only for men in their culture. This discrimination already began to be implemented many years ago in museums in Canada, whose female staff were not allowed to handle some objects belonging to Great Plains Indians, which resulted in complaints of censorship; likewise, in Australia, women voiced their discontent at the fact that in some museums certain indigenous items were only visible to 'senior male figures with kinship claims' (Watson, 2007: 12). Tabloids in New Zealand fuelled controversy in 2010 because of similar restrictions implemented at the museum Te Papa Tongarewa in Wellington, where visitors now are warned that in Maori culture certain sacred objects must be kept away from pregnant or menstruating women, who are given the choice of entering or not the room where they are kept (Alderton, 2014: 266–270). According to Andrea Witcomb, both the museum theory and the practice need to be revised to encourage debate instead of perpetuating 'a simplistic celebration and reinforcement of existing identities' (Witcomb, 2015: 321). This would also obviously apply to the latest generation of museums-memorials of the Holocaust or of the victims of dictatorships, genocide or terrorism: in front of overpowering testimonies of human brutality there is no room for equidistance nor for revanchism. Yet, our historical memory must project its critical approach onto the present time. Something very tactfully achieved by the POLIN Museum of the History of Polish Jews, inaugurated in 2013 on the site of the former Warsaw ghetto. Visitors are asked about current issues regarding anti-Semitism or the integration of Jews in Poland such as: 'Who creates Jewish culture and for whom?'

Overcoming the old dilemma between temple or forum, critical thought reformulates the museum as a public stage where society keeps reviewing its values. Controversies have long been accepted as unavoidable, perhaps not sought after or provoked, but inherent to our collective life and to the accountability of institutions to society where museums are no longer viewed as indisputable oracles, neither in the case of science and technology displays nor – above all – those of history and art (Harris, 1995; Boyd, 1999). Ethical problems regarding corporate patronage have become a main concern, arousing protests such as the *Liberate Tate* movement against sponsorship by the oil company BP. In any case, unlike other social forums where lobbying experts, opinionated journalists, circles of friends or private families are taking sides in hot issues, museums are supposed to be civic spaces unaligned with particular interests or ideologies (Casey, 2001). But the lack of alignment must never mean neutrality so that, while abiding by the appropriate legislation, museums must also be critically involved in questions of ideology, values and creeds, including matters of sex and gender, political disputes or social tribulations (Knell, MacLeod & Watson, 2007; Levin, 2010; Piotrowski, 2011; Sandell & Nightingale, 2012; Message, 2015: 271–273; Watson, 2015: 288). On the occasion of the 2015 refugees crisis in Europe, a silent protest demonstration went on for several weeks in Helsinki in front of the Ateneum Art Museum, whose director decided to display at the façade a huge work by graffiti artist EGS, *Europe's Greatest Shame #11*, a reproduction of which was displayed there again in 2017 when a change in legislation menaced refugees from Iraq, Somalia and Afghanistan with deportation, thus fuelling social controversies and solidarity reactions. Great museums may also publicly dissent from some governmental decisions to stress their institutional independence, as did the MoMA of New York in answer to the prohibition ordered by President Trump in 2017 denying entry to the USA to immigrants from seven Islamic countries: for months, in its galleries displaying the permanent collection, works by Picasso, Matisse and Picabia were replaced with pieces by Iraqi Zaha Hadid, Sudanese Ibrahim el-Salahi and several artists born in Iran 'to affirm the ideals of welcome and freedom as vital to this Museum, as they are to the United States' (John Reeve's speech, quoted in Knell, 2019: 60).

Critical museology is best defined by its inclination to tackle sensitive matters, being particularly predisposed to impugn hegemonic colonialist approaches persisting in an increasingly multicultural and globalised society (Padró, 2003; Lorente, 2012: 79). But controversial matters also call for controversial measures, revealing the existence of underlying conflicts 'staging a confrontation between conflicting positions' (Mouffe, 2013: 73–74). For instance, regarding the thorny issue of the restitution of cultural objects, it is good to publicly admit that unanimity does not exist amongst scholars. A majority of critical anthropologists sympathise with the demand to return certain human remains or objects of ritual value; many others, however, would rather consider each particular case individually. But there is unanimous consensus for the need to have the general public involved in this debate, which indicates that 'there are many forms of "critical" museological practices that could be tied to meaningful change' (Hasian & Wood, 2010: 134). Museums thus become not only the showcase for conflictive heritage but also of curatorial dilemmas, openly disclosing to visitors the contrasting visions of the world as elucidated in front of their eyes (Gómez Martínez, 2011; De Angelis, 2014; Schärer, 2018). The meta-discourse that seeks to attract visitors' attention towards curatorial work and its quandaries ought to be considered ultimately the most distinctive feature of self-proclaimed 'reflexive' or 'critical' museology inside museums. Those in university campuses had been, not by chance, leading the way.

By the same token, critical museologists have reached outstanding positions in university contexts. The celebratory tune of former museum studies has given way to critical revisions which have proliferated in courses and academic texts, including this book, whose first chapter already pointed out that many scholars have written about critical museology though each one gives it a peculiar name and perceives it differently depending on the respective language or discipline. It would thus seem suitable to end this second chapter ironically recalling such a controversial idiosyncrasy: if questioning is the principal feature of 'critical museology', the inherent misgivings attached to such a term must be revealed. As the terminological conundrum is obvious, my opinion about the matter must emphasise diverging pluralism and personal viewpoints both in terms of museological theory and of museographic praxis. The next chapter is dedicated to them.

Notes

1 On expressions of love/hate towards museums as an art genre, particular reference ought to be made to a pioneering compilation (Bronson & Gale, 1983), a large exhibition at New York's MoMA (McShine, 1999) and a major referential book (Putnam, 2001).
2 Coinciding with the Covid-19 pandemic, when online communication has been strengthened so much, the MNCARS has eventually installed a label with a QR code on its exterior facade in front of the work by Rogelio López Cuenca discussed here, but by mistake the information corresponds to his other piece, which instead has no identification label.
3 *Gallery 33: An Exhibition About The Way People Live* is the permanent exhibition of this municipal museum whose purpose is to show, from a critical viewpoint, the world's and Birmingham's cultural diversity; on the top floor of this Gallery, controversial temporary exhibitions are held. Abundant bibliography exists in this respect, listed in one of the best-known texts of the leading specialist Jane Peirson Jones, compiled in Hooper-Greenhill (1999: 258–274).

3 Variety and plurality in spatial and interpretive discourse

Figure 3.1 Banner with portrait of a curator with his comments in the first person on his favourite piece at the Pergamonmuseum in Berlin.

Source: Photo by J. Pedro Lorente, with kind permission from the museum

DOI: 10.4324/9781003263050-4

3.1 From the doctrinaire modern cube to postmodern museographical diversity

In the architecture of the second half of the twentieth century, the triumph of the International Modern Style brought about homogenised business districts in large cities around the world, both indoors and outdoors. Cultural buildings would sometimes be more idiosyncratic, after more than a century of archetypical neoclassical temples, but internally they also used to adopt a common cliché, especially in museums and modern art galleries throughout the Western world, all very similar to one another, even as regards their contents. If they did not have works by Picasso or Pollock, their vernacular emulations would be used. However, the narrative repeated in every country aped in both contents and displays the dogma of modernity revealed by the Museum of Modern Art in New York through a museographical epiphany based on white walls, with paintings hung very far apart, never superimposed, and each illuminated with an aura of artificial light along a compartmentalised path to guide visitors' steps according to the historic advance of styles and schools consecrated by the modern canon. The reference model was the permanent exhibition of MoMA's collection of paintings and sculptures set up by Alfred Barr Jr. in 1958 but rearranged by William Rubin in 1973 with even less ornamentation or furnishing, just a few benches, harder and narrower than the previous ones. Nothing invited dialogue and discussion with either accompanying persons or fortuitous seat companions; such string of windowless cubicles favoured a rather silent journey of secluded reverential contemplation. It is not surprising that this museum was compared to the Christian pilgrimage temples in a famous article by Carol Duncan and Allan Wallach, who described it as a sanctuary of modernity where the faithful had to walk devoutly absorbed following an initiation journey to receive the revelation of modern art (Duncan & Wallach, 1978).

This paradigm was already being questioned from multiple fronts and not only by those who criticised it on paper, who then coined the ironic nickname of 'white cube'.[1] In their professional practice, artists and curators also rebelled against such a standardised museography, venturing into other ways of showing art. They often experienced alternative displays in temporary shows and events associated with an underground creativity cultivated in the dereliction of raw industrial spaces; although more and more of that curatorial experimentalism was seeping into the smart settings of highbrow culture (O'Neill, 2016; Fernández López, 2020). An alternative counter-model to the paradigm consecrated by MoMA was tested in France under the leadership of Pontus Hultén, director of the Musée National d'Art Moderne and head of exhibitions at the Pompidou Centre in Paris, and inaugurated in 1977, whose strident architecture marked an urban landmark; but its interior also seemed a well of surprises. With beautiful views of the city and breaking away with the one-way pilgrimage encased between walls closed to natural light, the MNAM was a space with 'squares' and 'cabins' where visitors-flanêurs could venture, or not, depending on personal interests and could even activate some automated devices to bring down the pictures stored in vertical reserves called *cinacothèques*. Beaubourg seemed to be the architectural icon of a new era (Davis, 1990), very much in tune with demands for the popular participation pleaded by the *nouvelle muséologie*; nevertheless, it failed to meet expectations because as soon as Hultén left, the new managers commissioned a reform of the museum's interior in 1982 and returned to the 'white cube' prototype, with compartmentalised spaces in a grid along a central avenue. Curiously, its author was designer Gae Aulenti, who was then in charge of the musealisation of the former Orsay station in Paris, whose inauguration in 1986 once again marked another milestone in the deconstruction of the modern canon as this new museum of nineteenth-century art no longer focussed exclusively on the 'progress' of innovative art from Delacroix to Courbet, Manet, Impressionism and Post-Impressionism but offered cross-views of other tendencies like *pompier* art or Symbolism. Receptive to such interconnectivity, even MoMA had reformulated its museography in 1984 after the expansion of its headquarters by Cesar Pelli. The permanent exhibition of its sculptural and pictorial collection maintained the same itinerary of labyrinthine advance through rooms with correlative numbering; but visitors were no longer obliged to follow it as the former arrangement of a single entrance door and one exit door in each room was open to other possible viewing sequences. For example, by connecting Room 3, dedicated to Futurism, Expressionism and Fauvism, with Room 6, assigned to Suprematism and Constructivism, which in turn also led to Room 9, destined for Abstract Expressionism.

Other postmodern architecture landmarks were breaking the mould of a colourless and introverted museum pattern whose uniform reiteration would be challenged around the world by the exultant museum boom of very heterogeneous and surprisingly striking buildings, both internally and externally (Davis, 1990; Newhouse, 1998; Giebelhausen, 2003; Montaner, 2003; MacLeod, 2005). However, the crisis of the great narratives proclaimed by postmodern philosophers broke away from the chronological ordering of collections, such as that orchestrated by Rudi Fuchs at the Castello di Rivoli, open to the public since 1984 displaying artworks in a conceptual response to each space of the palatial frame, or the provocative selection of content devised by Jean-Christophe Ammann in the curiously coloured rooms designed by Hans Hollein for the Museum für Moderne Kunst in Frankfurt, which opened in 1991. From then onwards, the teleological narrative of modern art would be highly contested in many museums which, instead of being mere containers consecrated to the fervent adoration of believers, would echo hesitations in the face of the dilemma between direct experience of art with no imposed interference and/or a diversity of interpretive discourses (Serota, 1996; McClellan, 2008; McLuhan, Parker & Barzun, 2008). These institutions would no longer point out the univocal way to progress with their art holdings, but varied points of view in a changing selection of their collection, if they had it.

The success of relational aesthetics promoted by Nicolas Bourriaud at the turn of the millennium challenged passive attitudes of people in museums and art exhibitions; but no less influential was the claim staked by Jacques Rancière for an 'emancipated spectator', who autonomously builds his/her own itinerary. On a world scale, the Guggenheim Bilbao and the Tate Modern would be the paradigmatic examples of this museographical turn according to Charlotte Klonk, for whom three characteristics could be highlighted in synthesis, the first being the development of 'multiple narratives, not a single one of which represents a uniquely authoritative story' (Klonk, 2009: 206). In her view, the second greatest spatial novelty would be the optical and haptic connection of the museum with urban life, and the third the elimination of interior compartments to achieve greater dynamism during visits, instead of the monotonous succession of halts. These changes could be exemplified in different countries with new museums in either purposely built architectures or converted industrial buildings. Frank Gehry's glamourous edifice for the Guggenheim Bilbao inaugurated in 1997 and the iconic power station musealised in 2000 by the Tate Modern, set a trend in the renouncement of a predetermined interior route, the multiplication of visual connections with the urban environment and the encouragement of experimental synergies between contents and container.

All this falls in line with the critical theories about museums and heritage that emerged at the turn of the millennium, which advocate other practices that break away with modern paradigms. Urbanists now prefer museums with unconventional architecture, which generates idiosyncratic iconic visibility from the outside and, at the same time, allows visitors to let their sight to glimpse external views all around, such as the great panorama of San Francisco offered from the Young Museum, designed by Herzog and de Meuron and opened in 2005, or the multidirectional viewpoints offered by Zaha Hadid's National Museum of 21st-Century Art (MAXXI) in Rome, successfully exploited since its opening in 2009. Many other examples could be cited, but perhaps the most emblematic of critical museology pleas is the Acropolis Museum in Athens, designed by the Swiss-American Bernard Tschumi and his Greek partner Mijalis Fotiadis. Inaugurated in 2009, it is a museum and interpretation centre of the neighbouring archaeological complex, to which it not only opens up to stunning views but also functions as a beacon of light and a showcase of treasures visible from the outdoors by displaying to the eyes of the outside world its hoards as well as its lacks – of great political symbolism, to support the claim for the return of the Parthenon marbles preserved in the British Museum. Such visual interconnections have been paramount for Renzo Piano's glass-enclosed extension of the Art Institute of Chicago, inaugurated in 2009, with spectacular views of the skyline, but which also allows visibility from the outside of some art works and museum visitors. The same happens in the new building of the Whitney Museum of American Art in New York, also designed by Piano and inaugurated in 2015, which overlooks the Meatpacking District, transformed into an art district since the pedestrianisation of the High Line. This architect has done it again in Santander since 2017, with his iconic Centro Botín overlooking the bay and the city, with interconnected glances indoors/outdoors, following the precedent of the Parisian Centre Pompidou, its inevitable paragon in many ways (Lorente & Gómez, 2021).

Internally, the critical alternative to the white cube is less obvious as the most straightforward option would apparently be black cubicles, that is, dark rooms for video projections that have become ubiquitous in any contemporary art institution but are still rather isolated spaces of reclusive contemplation.[2] They can be found at both the Guggenheim Bilbao and the Tate Modern, but other museums have experimented more radical combinations of dark settings with multiple criss-crossing paths, albeit with mixed success. The murky labyrinthine structure created by Daniel Libeskind in his extension of the Jewish Museum in Berlin, opened in 1999 with the building still empty, was acclaimed worldwide for its originality, although many expectations fell short somewhat by the conventional arrangement of contents adopted after its inauguration in 2001, despite its assumed open narrative (Basu, 2007: 56). The sculptural Kunsthaus building, opened in Graz in 2002, had dark and wall-less exhibition rooms which have stimulated imaginative site-specific displays, but internal walls are often erected in order to host itinerant exhibitions. Another daring layout innovation came about with the Museum of Roman Art, inaugurated in 2005 by the city council of the Italian capital on the old Montemartini thermoelectric plant, whose old machinery is used as a spectral background scenery to install ancient sculptures from the Capitoline Museums and for contemporary site-specific art interventions, all of which have been interpreted as a bold critical alternative to the modern episteme (Janulardo, 2015). That was also the aspiration of the Parisian Quai Branly Museum, inaugurated in 2006, whose visiting route takes the form of a dark labyrinth, although it has been blamed of obscurely inducing a reverent homogeneous aestheticisation of its pieces from different cultures, instead of problematising the provocative contrasts that incite critical thinking (Clifford, 2007: 14; García Canclini, 2010: 138; Geismar, 2015: 187).

Indeed, regardless of scenographic clarity or darkness, the main issue lies in favouring dialogic spaces instead of immersive pilgrimages through rooms in enfilade, which mentally isolated visitors from the rest of the world in an ecstatic mindflow typical of a pilgrimage of psychic absorption that is almost incompatible with our current way of life, always diverted by mobile phones and social networks. It is true enough that these personal devices can mislead our attention, but they are also very useful for everyone to check data, to compare opinions, to exert more autonomously as critical agents and to give lay visitors a proactive and self-conscious role in museums, even in those of art, once catechisers of an axiomatic aesthetic devotion, which fortunately have been opening up to a greater diversity of beliefs and discourses (Warner, 2002). If art historians now like to write books in which the traditional dry and distant diachronic account yields to other more creative storylines (Elkins, 1997), the same happens with curators' narratives and their spatial discourses. Even New York's MoMA showed a temporary re-reading of its permanent collection in 2000 in non-chronological order under the title 'Modern Starts', a play of words that announced the forthcoming opening of the Yoshio Taniguchi-designed extension and, in the meantime, pondered a new starting point for modern art, much to the scandal of its regulars, who sighed with relief when in 2004 the enlarged building presented once again the canonical display ordered by chronology and styles, albeit with many more connecting doors between rooms (Psarra, 2009: 185–210).

It is well that it should be so because no one denies the convenience of preserving for posterity a display arrangement that already forms part of the heritage that this institution keeps as a sign of identity. Yet in other instances, long-established displays can be changed or combined with different exhibition modes. This is what the Thyssen Museum in Madrid has done since March 2011 in the room dedicated to the Russian avant-gardes, whose paintings almost cover the walls from top to bottom, as in some famous El Lissitzky exhibitions; indeed it seemed an incongruity to keep displaying them sparsely hung following the North American museum model of the white cube. Now nobody is shocked to find densely packed displays of pictures, as also seen in the neighbouring Museo Nacional Centro de Arte Reina Sofía, especially for photographs, which have been given greater prominence in the permanent display. Moreover, the highlights of the museum collection are spatially distributed in discontinuous sections torn apart in separate parts of the building, leaving the navigation through them up to visitors themselves. For instance, by the lift found on the second floor, discreet indicators stuck to the windows suggest the possibility of going to Picasso's *Guernica* by two alternative routes: either to the right following the path of Cubism or to the left through the rooms dedicated to Surrealism (Arias Serrano, 2015: 141). Linear flow is not a problem, if various paths are offered in a consistent frame, so that 'visitors can gauge what they want to focus on or visit' (Lindsay, 2016: 223). Museums have thus learned to treat their audiences as sovereign 'clientele' who are offered a personalised cultural experience (Rodney, 2019). Instead of correlatively numbered rooms, or a single route signposted with arrows on the wall, divergent or intersecting paths marked on the floor with bright coloured and tactile walkways, which are already common in airports, have been enthusiastically adopted by museum designers.

These open routes are not always feasible, especially in some museums with multitudes of tourists, where recommended itineraries have been marked for safety reasons to facilitate the flow of visitors or for other reasons. For example, due to Covid-19, one-way circuits have been re-imposed in 2020 by large institutions with massive attendances, including the Guggenheim Bilbao and the Tate Modern. Yet this does by no means imply a return to the teleological chronological-stylistic narrative because even after the adoption of a one-way route in times of pandemic, the counterpoint of aesthetic-thematic synapses has been maintained in the display of their respective permanent collections. Nevertheless, like all fashions, also the transhistorical re-readings of art collections might be declared outmoded soon or later. Since the 1980s, there have been uncountable cases of art galleries intermingling old masterworks in displays of contemporary art or vice versa, but such experiments have simply highlighted iconographic or formal pairings, often regarded as playful rearrangements by invited artists, not intending to definitely decry customary taxonomies in art institutions (Bawin, 2014: 155). It might have been fun to mix old and recent artworks, but still no one has dared to question so much the chronological divide to the extent of contesting the continued existence of museums that specialise in modern and contemporary art.

Rather than a total convolution, the tendency moves towards a cultural syncretism of various lineages (Hernández, 2015). The postmodern fascination with the *Wunderkammern* has not entailed the repudiation of later museographical patterns, but the re-appreciation of heteroclite juxtapositions of artistic pieces to be found in Ancien Régime palatial galleries and in many museums of the 19th and 20th centuries (Marín Torres, 2003). It was not so strange that Turner stipulated when bequeathing his works that two of his landscapes should be hung in the National Gallery in London together with two paintings by Claude Lorrain; a curious precedent that perhaps inspired at Tate Britain the pairing of an almost abstract painting by Turner with another by Rothko in the Clore Wing. Similar transhistorical confrontations had already been rehearsed in the permanent display of the Sainsbury Centre for the Visual Arts inaugurated in 1978 in Norwich on the

University of East Anglia campus, camouflaging the historic-artistic gaps in the collection by not presenting the selection in diachronic order but structuring it in visual correspondences between pieces from different times and places, such as the stylised sculptures of Giacometti and the archaic statues of the Cyclades Islands (Figure 3.2).

A strategy of transhistorical flow paths that has also proved very appropriate for the Tate Modern, inaugurated in 2000, where the great novelty in the display of the collection has been to allow plural itineraries 'treating the visitors as individuals with independent needs and wants' (Donnellan, 2018: 111). Far from trying to substitute one canonical discourse for another, its display articulation was defined as one of the many possible readings, which would be completely renewed after a few years. Indeed, the presentation has been periodically changed, gaining in radicality the proposed visual parallels and the revisionism of the display, which favours contrasts between sets of works from different periods and styles.

That has been a fundamental change. Nowadays, there are countless museums of modern and contemporary art that, following this trend, present the treasures of their collection in displays that are no longer called permanent but 'long-term temporary exhibitions', as they neither intend to be perennial nor try to reveal a fixed dogma, but test curatorial options by exploring various artistic constellations. They usually last about 3 years or

Figure 3.2 The Sainsbury Centre's *Living Area* featuring their collection.

Source: Photo by Andy Crouch; image courtesy of the Sainsbury Centre

even more, with subtle changes in individual works from time to time, but some institutions like Kiasma in Helsinki or Artium in Vitoria-Gasteiz regularly produce a total rearrangement of their selection every year, following different thematic threads. Others like Louisiana Museum in Humlebæk take a middle way by conventionally displaying great modern masterpieces from the collection in summer when many first-time tourists arrive while they surprise the regular local public with unexpected pairings in winter (Tzortzi, 2015: 215). These are experimental revisions that can bring out new rhizomatic connections by dismantling a historic narrative without attempting to instate instead another definitive paradigm.

Having replaced the uniformity of the ubiquitous white cube with very diverse display scenographies, an even more marked change is, thus, the transition from a top-down ever-lasting revelation to an autodidactic grasping of contingent interpretations. Critical museology encourages in this way phenomenological experiences of intellectual self-learning blurring pre-established hierarchies: all sorts of stuff can be found apparently mixed-up; although this makes the work of museum interpretation even more crucial. It should be borne in mind that, although there is often talk of putting artworks of different styles and periods in 'dialogue', two works of art do not speak to one another or to third parties, for the agents of this communication process are always humans. There are museums, such as Kolumba in Cologne or the Insel Hombroich Museum near Düsseldorf, in which texts are dispensed with, so that visitors can construct their own interpretations based on an 'aesthetic shock' (Gob & Drouguet, 2010: 129). However, some unexpected rearrangements can be very difficult to apprehend by the uninitiated public and even by connoisseurs, so there is a risk that these peculiar confrontations of exhibits will turn into scholarly winks shared only between colleagues, as warned by several authors who have examined this trend in a book eloquently entitled *The Transhistorical Museum* (Wittocx et al., 2018).

A very easy solution is to add indicative titles, labels, arrows, colour codes or other visual indicators in the museum's signage as a set of clues that lead to indicative trails, routes and readings – at various levels – and in such a way that visitors playfully ruminate their own way. Such is the strategy followed by the aforementioned example of Artium, the museum of modern and contemporary art inaugurated in 2002 in the Basque capital, Vitoria-Gasteiz, which annually changes its content and display of galleries by presenting a selection of its collection sorted into aesthetic-iconographic sections marked with differentiated colours and with keywords written in large letters at the tops of walls. This has not freed it from controversies, which have intensified in many other subsequent examples of challenging transhistorical 're-readings' of the respective collection, such as the rearrangement at the Galleria Nazionale d'Arte Moderna e Contemporanea in

Rome since 2016. Its director, Cristiana Collu, conceived this postmodern revamp in collaboration with a team of thinkers and artists by producing a title from Hamlet, 'Time is Out of Joint', plus successive temporary shows revising/contesting it, including one in 2019 with the ironically inverted title: 'Joint is out of Time'.

It is tempting to consider this experimental form of museography as being characteristic of contemporary art museums as they ought to be very much in tune with the latest trends in culture and creativity. Of course, these institutions have a stronger influence of typical twenty-first-century relational, situational, dialogic, participatory or interactive art forms, which are offering the public a more proactive role. This seems confirmed by the strategies of democratisation of access to art in two Australian museums, the Art Gallery of New South Wales and the Museum of Contemporary Art, analysed by Ien Ang (Ang, 2015: 216 and 222). Perhaps the best practice could be arranging display itineraries for visitors who want guidance but fostering free will and critical self-examination, in an exercise of institutional self-containment. It is true that contemporary art museums should be especially aware of reflecting – and making the public reflect – on what they show or what they do not as they manage a heritage that has not yet passed the judgement of history and are subject to more pressure from politicians, the market or any 'opinion maker'. Inexorably, the risk of making mistakes in their choices is higher, which means that a higher percentage of their acquisitions will remain stored in reserves, beyond public scrutiny (Tali, 2018).

Discerning what is shown to the public and what is stored in reserves is a professional responsibility that may well be shared with museum visitors or they should at least be aware of it. A good way to promote this awareness are visit trails that lead to semi-reserves or to warehouses accessible not only to a visiting expert but to anyone. This is a long-standing common feature in science museums, where experts like Richard Toon distinguish three modalities, each with its specific name: *peek-in*, when the public can see a storeroom but cannot enter it; *walk-in*, if visitors are allowed to enter but have to move around the glazed storage area; *walk-through*, where people circulate freely between duly protected showcases (Toon, 2010). Museologist and art historian Javier Gómez speaks with enthusiasm about these three options and celebrates the fact that all kinds of visual access to store areas are being implemented inside museums of art and antiquities, sometimes made visible even to passers-by from the street. According to him, this 'citizen's right' to know also the hidden face of public collections is still rare outside northern Europe and the Anglosphere (Gómez, 2016: 275–298). Australian architect and designer William Smart goes further and claims for institutions that are not only transparent, even in political terms, but are also more open and invites society to enter and reflect on what remains behind the scenes in museums (Smart, 2020). Isn't that a great way to put critical museology into practice in museums?

3.2 Participatory communication, personal voices and metadiscursive interpellations

It is all well that the museum visit no longer functions as a catechetical pilgrimage; yet not only the modern 'white cube' has become obsolete but also any kind of educational discourse devoted to cultural indoctrination. Specially after the reconsideration by Michel Foucault of the archaeology of knowledge and Bruno Latour's reinterpretation of the sociology of sciences from the theories of the actor-network, which brought about a cultural context where no discipline recognised objective knowledge or absolute truths. The desirable praxis in museums of any specialty should be to leave behind old paradigms of civilisation contested from a post-colonial perspective and admitting 'the highly contingent nature of the interpretations offered' (Karp & Lavine, 1991: 7). Hence, museologists at the turn of the millennium shifted their attention to relative interpretations and narratives producing a non-authoritarian or at least non-dogmatic communication process, wherein even discordant interpretations would be echoed (Davallon, 1992; Hooper-Greenhill, 2000; Duncan, 2002; MacDonald, 2003; Witcomb, 2003).

There seemed to be an emergent universal consensus on the rejection of institutional discourses that used to restrict museums to the role of impersonal transmitters of incontestable axioms emanating from high above. Power relations could no longer be exercised or assented according to the vertical principle of authority formerly assumed, both inside and outside museums. Leaving behind a modern canon of art-historical narrative, artworks more and more often would be displayed in 'visual dialogues' with multiple readings, giving visitors the power to make their own conjectures about formal affinities, thematic relationships, or other personal considerations. Similarly, science and technology museums got used to show divergent conjectures or challenging theories from heterodox approaches. Breaking with the inertia that had turned museums into resonance boxes of the dominant *pensée unique*, the general move was for anonymous discourse to be superseded by signed and personal messages, as Elaine Heumann Gurian pointed out:

> Unsigned exhibitions reinforce the notion that there is a godlike voice of authority behind the selection of objects. But presenting a curator as an individual usefully demonstrates that exhibitions are in reality like signed columns rather than new releases and that each producer, like each columnist, has a point of view.

(Gurian, 1991: 187)

Such tendency would lead critical museologists to encourage plural inter- pretations combining sanctioned perspectives with emerging contestations gaining ground (Padró, 2003; Reese, 2003; Macdonald, 2006: 3). 'Mono- glossy', that is, categorical statements expressing a single point of view should be replaced by 'heteroglossy', following a terminology coined by the Russian literary theorist Mikhail Bakhtin, from whom an ICOFOM sympo- sium borrowed also the adjective 'dialogic', a qualifier potentially applicable to any museum aware of the existence of different personal criteria (Des- vallées & Nash, 2011). Discourses would gain legitimacy from dialectical argumentations considering other people's standpoints, both in museum the- ory and practice. Numerous museologists have enthusiastically greeted this tendency to present a wide range of voices, values and experiences, visibilis- ing subjectivities, personal stories and opposing points of view (Whitehead, 2005: 89, 118; Henning, 2006: 154; Hooper-Greenhill, 2007: 82; Holo & Álvarez, 2009: 56, 75; Marstine, 2013; Semedo, 2020: 125).

This commitment to subjectivity can be noted especially in social history museums, where it is a common policy to include some personal testimo- nies, such as photos/films and sound or written statements of intellectuals, workers, emigrants, soldiers, victims of the holocaust or from a dictator- ship, survivors of the Titanic or other individuals of any kind with whom visitors may subjectively identify.[3] Some of the most celebrated examples in museum studies bibliography are the Museum of New Zealand-Te Papa Tongarewa (Schorch, 2013) and the Melbourne Museum after the inaugura- tion in 2013 of its Bunjilaka Gallery (Witcomb, 2015) for their interactive screens and audio points where we can come across personal statements or interviews with a diversity of people. Other more recent studies prefer to focus on wireless technological resources, such as audio guides – now downloadable on our own mobile phones – or websites offering podcasts, commented visits or other speeches that also present a plurality of voices and points of view, although their users manipulate them in solitary isola- tion, which is not exactly a step forward in the line of argument that I am trying to develop here. In order to get in contact with other people's points of view, it seems better to look, read, express curiosity, listen, manoeuvre levers and press buttons together with other human beings.

It is not enough to bear witness of the growing plurality in museum discourses. The next step forward should be to interrelate and even estab- lish some kind of dialogue involving people with different professional perspectives and points of view, as has been explored in collaborative and/ or relational art (Kester, 2004; Fernández & Río, 2007; Raunig & Ray, 2009). Far ahead of the game are some science and technology museums such as the San Francisco Exploratorium, which was a pioneer in on-site demonstrations of interactive edu-communication offered by explainers to casual groups of visitors and now is encouraging these mediators to also promote socialising talks through Internet with great success according to Nina Simon, who has also pointed out other examples, such as the New York Hall of Science and five other American museums that in 2004 installed a device called Haptic Arm Wrestling allowing anyone to trial strength with another totally unknown user in an institution from a different city (Simon, 2010: 57, 99). They therefore avoid isolating visitors individually in the management of a technological resource, offering relational devices that have to be manipulated between two or more persons, who are granted the opportunity to engage with different human beings. Many other co-participation strategies that open opportunities for interpersonal connection have been reported by Nina Simon in her excellent book *The Participatory Museum*, although it is striking that these are almost always initiatives carried out in temporary exhibitions, educational workshops or other transitory activities (cf. also Patterson, 2021). Much better would be to highlight participatory activities perennially incorporated in interpretations of the permanent collection, by means of traditional comment boards or new technological devices inviting visitors to share their own thoughts and life experiences, as I have seen in the National Numismatic Museum of Mexico, the Museum of Independence in Bogotá or the Vancouver Museum, where anyone can write his/her own arguments for others to read them, preferably next to the showcases that have elicited these comments. It is something similar to the typical 'Write Your Own Label' contests inviting the public to write captions, bestowing selected texts with the honour of being placed for a time next to the official label (Nashashibi, 2003), yet the most enthusiastic supporters of this participatory endeavour would like to have no solution in continuity regarding such personal collaborations with members of the public, who should be co-constructing content and stories in museums on a permanent basis (García Fernández, 2015: 44).

Ultimately, the key to success of this subjective exegetical interaction lays in the hands of museum professionals, some of which have a long experience in animating/filtering such interpretive confrontations. Society museums are particularly well used to tell stories shared by their visitors, who can even donate personal objects as testimony of their biographical comments, as is the case of the Museum of Broken Relationships in Zagreb or the Musée National de l'Histoire de l'Immigration in Paris. These ways of emphasising the subjectivation of the museum discourse put us in contact with other individuals, turning the museum into a multivocal public space (Leite, 2012). But much as personal comments seem to flow spontaneously, there is a discreet professional arbitration work on which good results depend, a difficult task even for the most experienced staff, who can sometimes disappoint our expectations, according to museologist Jennifer Harris, referring to the Tenement Museum in New York, where all staff members must take turns leading oral visits, which usually culminate in a chat room with tea and cookies (Harris, 2011: 94). Those neighbourhood museums, together with the ecomuseums, were favourite testing ground for the *nouvelle muséologie* and its community-centred vindications which, abolishing the traditional division of roles in the museum between producers, interpreters and consumers of cultural heritage, would instigate global collaborative practices instead. However, their 'collective' provisos have been somehow questioned lately.

> These policies tend to vest authority in anointed chiefs and elders. But how many and which tribal members need to subscribe to the traditional view for it to remain authoritative? What about those who disagree? And about those who want to change this, or challenge it from within? Such strictures pertain to traditional indigenes and minorities, those now deemed to speak with one voice, but do they always do so? It becomes difficult for groups to modernize or change if they want to.
> (Jenkins, 2016: 264)

What is a community and who can speak on its behalf? It is time to reconsider social participation in a less gregarious way. This has been tested at the Museum of Anthropology at the University of British Columbia, which had a long tradition of collaboration with indigenous peoples, but under Anthony Shelton's leadership not only old tribal chiefs but also young men and women were invited to collaborate in the display of the Multiversity Galleries, whose interpretive boards transmit their respective personal comments, giving the name and photographic portrait of each interlocutor. For example Michael Willi, a young man from the Haida nation, who suggested to exhibit some potlatch masks but keeping one wrapped on a trunk in order to convey his mixed feelings about seeing in a prestigious museum these ceremonial items that, according to their religious rites, should be hidden when not in use (Figure 3.3). It is an extremely interesting reflection on the dilemmas that musealisation processes can elicit and perhaps also a peculiar way for those in charge of the museum to vicariously transmit these predicaments, through other people's statements. A comparable approach, with participatory and highly personal curatorial interpretations, has been adopted at the Asian, pre-Columbian and Hispanic art galleries of the Denver Art Museum, implementing since the last decade of the twentieth century a collaborative programme with the targeted communities involved so that their own comments are quoted on the information panels and in the audio guides; but the name of the respective author appears in all explanations, both *in situ* and on

Figure 3.3 A wrapped Haida mask in a showcase, with interpretation text by a young Haida at MoA, Vancouver.

Source: Photo by J. Pedro Lorente, with kind permission from the museum

the web, especially since the hiring in July 2019 of Dakota Hoska, a member of the Sioux tribe, as assistant curator of native arts.

In art museums, this kind of personal elucidation is often provided by artists, since their subjective comments would also offer the idiosyncratic point of view of someone intimately involved. It is reasonable for the public to be particularly interested in the explanations about artworks given by their authors, commonly offered in many contemporary art museums, featuring written statements and sound or audiovisual recordings. Some, such as the Pompidou Centre and the Tate Liverpool, have furthermore prioritised candidates with Fine Arts training when recruiting guide-interpreters, assuming they have a special ability to communicate their personal sensitivity to their listeners. Other museums aim even higher in this tactic of enlisting artists as mediators, giving *carte blanche* to famous painters, sculptors or filmmakers to choose a particular selection of favourite pieces from the collection and sharing their personal comments in recordings, wall texts and even in printed catalogues. Most memorable antecedents go back, for example, to *Raid the Icebox*, an exhibition mounted by Andy Warhol in 1969/1970 commissioned by the museum of the Rhode Island School of Design, which in turn inspired the *Artist's Choice* series of exhibitions developed since 1989 by New York's MoMA and emulated in many other institutions; yet many other historical milestones could be pointed out in the professional development of an emerging star of the contemporary art system: the 'artist-curator' in charge of temporary exhibitions or even original reconfigurations of some permanent rooms (Bawin, 2014: 142, 158; Green, 2018; Fernández López, 2020).

For decades, museum communication strategies that use a famous person as an inspiring 'guest star' have also been very common. His or her convening power can be considerable, as demonstrated by the large influx of visitors to the *Memoires d'aveugle* exhibition organised in 1990 by the Louvre, whose director had invited the philosopher Jacques Derrida with a spicy conceptual game to draw up the plan – *dessein* – of an exhibition of drawings – *dessins* – whose success led the Department of Graphic Arts to chain a series of exhibitions, under the generic title of *Parti Pris*, devised by other world-famous cultural mandarins. In the same way, notable people on a more local scale have been invited later by different institutions, such as the Galleria Civica d'Arte Moderna e Contemporanea in Turin, to celebrate its 150th anniversary rearranging in 2014 its collection according to four thematic arguments – Infinity, Speed, Ethics, Nature – respectively, as suggested by a philosopher, a businessman, an architect and a politician, all well-known personalities in the region; or the Bilbao Fine Arts Museum, which in 2018 reorganised all the rooms arraying its collection by alphabetically ordered terminological concepts, proposed by Kirmen Uribe, a Basque writer who had won the National Prize for Literature.

No less frequent is inviting a public figure to comment on his or her favourite museum piece. The collaboration of an actor, singer, athlete or 'influencer' in the broadest sense of the term can attract new audiences and make many more people pay attention to interpretive comments. An excellent proof can be found in the educational project carried out since the opening of the Tate Modern in 2000, ingeniously called 'The Bigger Picture': it consists of complementing the anonymous institutional label of certain artworks featured in the display of the permanent collection with another caption signed by a celebrity, like musician Brian Eno, writer AS Byatt or others. It is a pity that each year previous captions *d'auteur* are withdrawn to renew this educational campaign; had them been left there permanently, all rooms would be overflowing with very personal interpretive texts. Some are of special interest to critical museology, since they convey opinions that institutional texts might not dare to express. As is also the case with the 'Art Gallery Trail' programme launched in 2008 at the Norwich Castle Museum, where some art works from the permanent collection come with interpretive captions bearing the name, photo and profession of some well-known personalities with connections to East Anglia, from a racing driver or a novelist to photographer Mark Cator, whose comment on a Henry Bright's painting depicting a Norfolk landscape with St. Benedict's Abbey in ruins lashes out at the 'security fencing' placed today by business-people who speculate with territorial patrimonialisation. In the same vein, at the Museo de Navarra sensitive topics such as death, the female condition or social conscience have been boldly tackled for the *Complicidades/Konplizitateak* programme of interpretive itineraries offering since 2019 comments on some selected works written by local people of different professional profiles, printed in colourful illustrated brochures freely available (Arriaga & Aguirre, 2020).

Further external commentators collaborating regularly with art institutions and exhibitions are art historians and critics, whose services range from authenticating and appraising artworks to curating exhibitions, giving public lectures and divulgation talks or delivering scholarly essays for publications, explanatory brochures, audio guides, interpretation panels, etc. Given the difficulty often experienced by the general public with the latest trends in art, it seems a good idea to resort to professional experts in the galleries of contemporary art museums. Such is the firm commitment of the Musée d'Art Contemporain du Val-de-Marne (MAC-VAL) which, in collaboration with the French national section of the International Association of Art Critics, has been implementing with commendable persistence since 2005 the programme *C'est pas beau de critiquer?* The ironic title is a colloquial play on words that invites visitors to follow the personal interpretations of some masterpieces in the collection commented by members of AICA-France. Their comments are delivered to the public in two successive stages: firstly in a personal talk, which is usually scheduled every two or three months in days of free admission, when visitors can meet a prominent art critic in front of his/her chosen artwork, sometimes with the presence of its author; then, a quarter-fold folio-format brochure is published, on the back of which there is simply the institutional catalogue entry alongside a large colour photography of the selected masterwork while the front face features the name of the critic and his/her text, headed by biographical data about the artist. These brochures are available in dispensers placed next to each commented artwork, as a supplement to both its official label and room panels, thus serving as a counterpoint to the anonymous institutional discourse in the rooms dedicated to the permanent collection. Over the years, MAC-VAL has also compiled some of these illustrated essays in two bilingual English-French books. Many more examples could be cited, since other, museums such as the Centro de Arte Dos de Mayo (CA2M) in Móstoles, also commissioned art critics to select their favourite artworks from the collection, publishing their comments in the form of a printed catalogue, freely available on their website.

However, it is not enough to engage professional art critics; a further step towards critical museology would be to adopt the most peculiar characteristic of art criticism which, as Baudelaire used to say, is always personal and subjective. In general, referring to art presupposes a point of subjectivity, even in public museums, where supposedly it would be advisable to avoid demarcating official preferences in matters of taste, belonging to the sphere of personal choice. However, freedom of expression has certain limits for those who operate from an institutional platform, thus both external and especially internal curators have to carefully measure their words, especially in some political contexts around the world where messages contrary to governmental doctrines can motivate the withdrawal of an exhibition or even the closure of the museum (Marstine & Mintcheva, 2021). Nevertheless, these limits to individual opinions, previously assumed in silence, raise now many controversies in our museological context, in which museum professionals are encouraged to be more outspoken, not hiding behind institutional anonymity or vicariously transferring their opinions through the statements of invited personalities or partaking visitors.

Yet most of the texts and phrases found in museums are usually anonymous, emanating from a supra-personal cultural instance. We do not know who is addressing us or by what authority. Of course, this is not the case with oral talks, workshops and guided tours, but the most common sources of information in museums are written texts: labels, room panels and even resting points with further reading, printed or electronic. The wordings are rather laconic in some art museums favouring a discreet modesty in the intermediation work, because there are still those who think that works of art speak for themselves. But art institutions cannot completely relinquish their educational responsibility, championing the 'whatever' interpretation as the final and desired outcome (Meszaros, 2006: 13). Nor should they overwhelm with an excess of informative texts, which could be perceived as an interference, as it was said in 2007 about the new presentation in the permanent rooms of the Detroit Institute of Arts (Chambers, 2009). Now, since many art museums have dismantled the traditional presentation by styles or schools to propose novel 're-readings' of the collection according to personal criteria, the least that can be expected is that they offer clues explaining their plots and idiosyncratic pairings of works, not always obvious to other people (Carrier, 2006: 103).

This was assumed by the Tate since they began in 1991 to rearrange their galleries each year with puzzling transhistorical displays, for which precise instructions on interpretive texts were delivered and kept at the information desk of Tate Britain in a set of green files that were accessed by staff members, including Sylvia Lahav who was working at Tate before becoming lecturer at Goldsmiths College. She then believed that although the reign of arrogance of the 'white cube' had ended, it was not necessary to blindly follow 'along the path of over-interpreting everything' (Lahav, 2000: 22); but in her doctoral thesis she acquiescently documented (Appendix E) successive Guidelines for gallery texts compiled in 2006 and 2008 that advocated giving a more human touch to labels, possibly identified with their authors' signature or byline, something requested in an internal document entitled Interpretation at Tate Modern (Appendix D) also reproduced, with small variations, in another closely related doctoral thesis and in subsequent publications out of it:

> Wall texts give an explanatory overview of the contents of the room. They will be written by the curator of the display, appearing with their byline. Including the curator's name is a way of avoiding the idea of a single 'authorial' voice for the Tate. It allows scope for a more informal approach and different points of view. It is also more honest about the fact that we are presenting ideas rather than answers.
>
> (*Interpretation Policy*, p. 9; apud Arriaga, 2010)

Amaia Arriaga, lecturer at the Public University of Navarra, has always supported as a fundamental claim of critical pedagogy that interpretation should be delivered in the first person. A previous fighter in Spain against the inertia of anonymous institutional discourse was Professor Teresa Sauret, who assumed in 2007–2013 the direction of the Municipal Heritage Museum of Málaga and had explanatory boards placed on each floor bearing the name of the respective authors of texts: some had been commissioned from external experts and others had been written by staff members, but all panels were signed. Unfortunately, they were eliminated as soon as she left the institution and the same happened at the National Museum of Fine Arts in Santiago de Chile, which in 2009 had been a pioneering example in identifying the names of people in charge of interpretation, be them museum staff or external guests, during the programme 'Exercises with the collection, on the Border' implemented by Ramón Castillo Inostroza, then Assistant Director and now a lecturer at the Diego Portales University. That programme was quickly discontinued and the same happened to the gallery of the New Kingdom of Granada (1550–1810) set up in 2011 on the second floor of the National Museum of Bogotá, with plenty of interrogative and critical interpretations on the wall panels, signed either by museum staff or external specialists. Given the hapless fate of all these short-lived examples, which I once greeted as exponents of critical museology (Lorente, 2015: 125–127), I am almost afraid to bring a bad omen to the Museum of Warsaw if I praise it here for systematically stating since 2017 the names of the writers of absolutely all its interpretive panels, starting with the wall poster introducing the permanent exhibition, entitled *Rzeczy warszawskie* – The Things of Warsaw, signed by Jrosław Trybus, who already lost in February 2019 his position as deputy director of the museum, recovering it by court decision in July 2020.

Recognition of authorship is a right assumed in all scientific contexts and it should also be part of best practices set up in museums.[4] It does not seem fair that, unlike current procedures in laboratories and research teams at universities or other scientific institutions, museum catalogue entries and interpretive texts remain anonymous, as it is the case with most of the curatorial work in museums. If curators reveal innovative interpretations and even personal ideas out of norm, giving them individual recognition should be a just cause according to critical museology (Padró, 2011); especially to the extent that it is a way of promoting critical thinking and reflection in/about the museum itself (Guzin-Lukic, 2017: 119). Indeed, museum texts could disclose not only the names of their authors but even their faces! There are many North American museums presenting at the entrance a few words of greeting and photos of the staff or distinguished employees of the month, as it is there a common marketing policy applied in the management of establishments of all kinds. Rarer is to find such human faces featuring along museum texts in galleries displaying the permanent collection. Although there are encouraging exceptions, even in Europe, it was a surprise for me to find in 2019, when visiting the Pergamon Museum in Berlin, a life-size full-length portrait of its metal restorer Gert Jendritzki with his statements in quotation marks explaining in the first person, both in German and English, the ingenious hinge system used by Egyptian scribes for some ivory boards shown in the adjoining display case. He had been chosen as one of the protagonists of the programme *Mein Lieblingstück* – My favourite object of the Staatlichen Museen zu Berlin (Figure 3.1).

In online dissemination, strategies there is also an increasing commitment to these personalised communication policies, which were considerably boosted during the 2020 confinement, for example, with the activity entitled *El Prado contigo/The Prado with you*, which published the comments of, among others, the museum director, speaking to the camera from home, without a tie. Similarly, Mauritshuis curator

Geert-Jan Borgstein delivered a series of 'Mini lectures from home' available at the museum website, commenting each week a different masterwork, chosen by the public on Facebook and Instagram. A direct personal connection was the key to success. It should be advised that community managers in charge of interacting with the public through museum blogs or social networks express themselves in the first person, signing their posts with their names. Perhaps this could help addressing the problem of unidirectionality in such communications, where most commonly people only respond with emoticons or with brief trivial comments (Rodríguez Ortega, 2011: 29). It would be great for museums to use technological resources to interact not just with mere virtual consumers but rather with active collaborators involved in curatorial functions and choices (Whitehead, 2012: 139).

New York's MoMA led a new way to on line participation in 2005 by uploading on its website podcasts of the official audio guide – with comments from the museum director and curators, artists or external experts – plus other allocutions sent by Internet users: anyone could propose a personal comment on his/her favourite artwork to be posted so that it might be listened by everybody. In 2014, the Museum of Contemporary Art of Barcelona went further, inviting whoever wanted to send proposals for virtual itineraries interrelating pieces from the collection; in fact, most of the online tours that were posted on its website had not been prepared by museum staff but by members of the public eager to have a try at curatorial/educational interpretation of art. In this way, some museums are parading their collections and socially showcasing curatorship as well, so as to make evident the human factor underpinning their professional tasks: the function of these institutions is not only to display art but also to expose the subjective reconsiderations about art (Ang, 2015: 216 and 222).

Notes

1 Although 'white cube' is sometimes translated into other languages, it has become a common expression worldwide preferably uttered in English, a language in which there were initially other variants, such as 'white box'. However, the prevailing designation was definitively consecrated by the book in which Brian O'Doherty compiled several articles under the title *Inside the White Cube* (O'Doherty, 1986).
2 In parallel to the 'white cube', the expression 'black box' or 'black cube' was coined to designate an equally neutral and closed space, but with dark walls and ceiling, traditionally used for aesthetic displays of jewels, treasures and even anthropological pieces, as in some exhibitions made famous since the 1960s by George-Henri Rivière, related to theatrical scenography.

3 It is a communication strategy so widespread that it is even used with fictional characters, in museums where we find, for example, the figure of a Celtic warrior or a medieval lady telling us what her life was like.

4 The recognition of authorship to the curators of temporary exhibitions is already something common in any type of institution, also in museums, even when they are staff members; in fact, their names are often made visible in the opening credits placed well visible in museum rooms that present selections from their collection conceptualized as a 'temporary' show, even if its duration is intended to last for many years, as occurs for example in the Museum of Modern Art of Mexico. But when a 'redisplay' of the permanent collection is presented, it is not usually stated in writing who has carried out this curatorial task.

4 Representations of historical legacies in times of self-reflexive museology

Figure 4.1 A display about the museum founding period in the atrium Paul Rivet of the *Musée de l'Homme*, Paris.

Source: Photo by J. Pedro Lorente, with kind permission from the museum

DOI: 10.4324/9781003263050-5

4.1 Museography as heritage: critical retrieving of historic displays

Postmodern interest in self-referential narratives brought about a general awareness of the need to focus public attention on not only what museums show but also on how they do it, according to their own curatorial strategies (Shelton, 1990: 99). The museum could no longer be conceived as a syntactically neutral container that supposedly should go unnoticed at the service of its contents. Visitors, thus, would develop curatorial consciousness while museum professionals became concerned that they should conserve, study, exhibit and interpret not just the collections in their care but also certain idiosyncratic arrangements and iconic resignifications, which can be a valuable cultural legacy as well. While modernity exalted novelties, in many ways postmodernity would time and again obsessively come to terms with heritages from the past. As Svetlana Alpers wrote, a new perspective came to reappreciate museums which retain outdated modes of exhibition, as testimonies of past ways of seing, not necessarily implying that 'they were wrong and we can get it right' (Alpers, 1991: 31). Considered from that point of view, an old-fashioned museum would acquire a 'metamuseum' value which, according to Mieke Bal, 'forbids its dismantling and prescribes its preservation for the sake of historical awareness' (Bal, 1992: 562). The museification of museums turned out to be a universal quandary discussed by many theoreticians, sometimes with inspired metaphors: 'Like the strata on an archaeological site, the museum today displays the various layers of its own history. At the core is the collection, surrounded by the vestiges of former modes of display as well as the architecture's own history' (Schubert, 2000: 132).

Indeed, just as Heraclitus' river, museums might seem permanent while they continuously change. Even historic houses or old galleries, zealously kept by curators specialising in the history of collecting, have somehow been inevitably renovated by introducing electricity and other modern conveniences. Nevertheless, they are increasingly more appreciated by the general public as Borgesian mirrors showcasing cultural treasures and reflecting past gazes while at the same time they echo the ravages of bygone years. Although some museum founders, like John Soane or Isabella Stewart Gardner, had given strict instructions to maintain everything unchanged, both the collection and the building have always endured alterations due to unforeseen events which, for some people, represent added charm, whereas normal wear and tear have required conservation or repair interventions, and sometimes total renewal or complete restoration from scratch. Museographical redos are nothing new but have become today a hot issue in critical heritage studies.

Archaeologists had resorted to the anastylosis of historic sites since the early nineteenth century while architects were rebuilding monuments long before the romantic 'restorations' à la Viollet-le-Duc that set the pace for the massive re-erection of edifices and historic quarters in Central Europe after the two World Wars. Bombed façades of many museums and exhibition centres then returned to their original state, but all fixtures inside were freely adapted to the latest developments in museum architecture. Thereafter, the fascination for recreated testimonies of former displays has only increased, very often entailing place dislocations. Most special cases were facsimile replicas of memorable modernist shows, reproduced both in permanent galleries and temporary exhibitions.[1] Obviously, their motivation was not properly architectural conservation but a homage to some experimental arrangement of avant-garde art deserving special pre-eminence in collective memory. Exceptionally, even in the greatest museums, whose founders never intended to preserve everything as a historical setting for posterity, there have also been momentous recoveries of their original displays, as in the case of the conscious restitution of the entire Galleria Palatina in Florence in the early 1990s, followed by many other cases.

Postmodern nostalgia of the past brought the ensuing overreaction. In an epoch of fashionable 'historicism' in art and architecture, many museums followed the vogue for a creative revival of *vintage* museographies promoted with the label 'historic hung'. That was the designation invoked in the 1980s and 1990s for cluttered displays of pictures on colourful clothed walls, first adopted by the Fitzwilliam Museum in Cambridge, the Manchester Art Gallery and the National Gallery of Scotland in Edinburgh (Clifford, 1982). It soon became a global trend, when the National Gallery in London and many other picture galleries across the world followed suit, although the typical reddish and densely crowded settings were not everywhere inspired in documented precedents (Klonk, 2009: 192). More accurate was the proper historicism of the 'surgical restorations' eliminating dropped ceilings at the National Gallery of London to recover the sculptural decoration and gilded inscriptions of the Octagon Hall and vestibules (Smith, 2007); nevertheless, as Christopher Whitehead pointed out, in this case modern additions were lost in order to return to Victorian décor, thus even such meticulous restitutions raised difficult questions of integrity and identity of historic heritage, as long as some episodes of the museum's history were deleted to recover others (Whitehead, 2012b: 166). Anyhow, the vogue for highly chromatic silk fabrics went perhaps too far, being emulated even in Madrid by the Prado, where they had never existed before. Such arbitrary refurbishment of old masters galleries in Victorian style decoration understandably raised disapproving comments, endorsed by Javier Gómez

Martínez, while this prominent critical museologist has more benevolently described similar decorations at the Metropolitan Museum of Art in New York, the Art Gallery of Ontario in Toronto or other institutions where these imitations of *Salon*-style exhibitions featured mainly academic nineteenth-century art, which could somehow justify an assimilation to 'period rooms' (Gómez Martínez, 2016: 229 and 231–234).

Another way of returning to historic museographies with more archaeo-logical rigour had been remarked by James Sheehan, prestigious historian of German museums, arguing that 'among the significant artefacts that museums contain are the intellectual, institutional, and architectural traces of their own history, residues of their own past' (Sheehan, 2000: 189). As practical substantiation of the latter point, the Nationalgalerie in Berlin, whose building underwent an ambitious campaign of works for its 125th anniversary, reopened in 2001 with a small room – Saal 1.04 – discreetly left unchanged, keeping its original mosaic floor, marble columns and dark green stucco wall. Still now a Raffael statue made in 1877 by Ernst Julius Hähnel stands in the middle as a memento of the former hall for sculptures, whereas a bust by Alexander Zschockke portraying Ludwig Justi pays hom-age to the museum director who set up the displays in 1910–1914. Other documents in showcases and framed photos recall further details of the history of the institution. Hence this sort of 'time capsule' is not only a memorial of a singular room of the former building but also a condensed institutional autobiography, just as an illuminated sign at the entrance explicitly declares: 'Geschichte der Nationalgalerie'.

A close but very different example is to be found at the Neues Museum in Berlin after its 'archaeological restoration' in 2009 by architect David Chipperfield, who recovered its old interior decorations as well as some antique showcases, especially at the famous *Roter Saal* – a name derived from the Pompeian red colour of the walls – which was the main room of the royal cabinet of prints founded by Friedrich Wilhelm IV, now display-ing some original collections of the Museum für Vor- und Frühgeschichte. Thus, in this case the interior architecture, wall paint and furniture have been replicated, but now the exhibits have nothing to do with the original museum contents. Indeed, many of the historic ornaments purposely made as a suitable décor for certain collections are no longer matching present museum displays; instead, these picturesque iconographies tell us their own history, which could be assimilated to self-assertive narratives inserting a story within a story, which in critical theory is usually called *mise en abyme*. At this point, the museum is exhibiting itself and remembering its past but emphasising its transformations. It is what the Prado is doing now in the former restroom of Ferdinand VII, where a temporary exhibition recreated in 2019 the contents of this cabinet intended for the king who founded the museum, whose original WC is kept there, but the paintings on display and the use of this room have changed.

In this sense, a more liberal yet congruent strategy regarding the museographical reinterpretation of recovered architectural remains was launched in Hagen, a propos the legacy of the Folkwang Museum founded in the early twentieth century by Karl Ernst Osthaus. Its empty building had become again an art museum after World War II nostalgically aiming to recover its former lustre. That ambition led to the restoration in the 1990s of the original Henry van de Velde *art nouveau* interior as the heart of the rebaptised Karl Ernst Osthaus Museum; but, of course, the collection did not match the original contents, which generated a tricky *musealisierung* dilemma (Crane, 1997), defiantly solved by the then director, Michael Fehr, who passionately argued for a 'responsive or reflective hanging' (Fehr, 2000: 50–51). Switching from primeval modernity to contemporary revisionism, that space was thus offered to related installations by living artists to establish creative historical connections with Osthaus' avant-garde impulse. Unlayering former structures and revealing their politics of representation in a reflexive museum was then the plan launched in 2003 at the Haus der Kunst in Munich by its director, Chris Dercon, coining the label *kritischer Rückbau* [critical reconstruction] (Rectanus, 2020: 57). Afterwards in Łódź (Poland), the Muzeum Sztuki decided to also use its reconstructed Neoplastic Room – a space originally designed by modern painter Władysław Strzemiński – as a catalyst for reinterpretations and reflections by contemporary artists, which has been the aim of the *Open Composition* programme carried out there since 2010 (Lorente, 2021). President of ICOMOS, Gustavo Araoz, would argue likewise that some tolerance of changes should be adopted in architectural conservation criteria in order to allow continuity of use, a proposal which was acknowledged as a new paradigm in critical heritage studies (Araoz, 2011; Witcomb & Buckley, 2013).

However, a different museum progeny would symbolically retrieve historic legacies no longer identified with a building and its architectural fittings but with some museographical setting recognised as a peculiar historical heritage. It is what the Museum of Warsaw does in its Room of Architectural Details, which is a symbolic postmodern reminder of the celebrated Lapidarium created by architect and curator Stanisław Żaryn in the 1960s (Figure 4.2). Another of my favourite examples is the *Gabinetto Segreto* [Secret Cabinet] in the National Archaeological Museum of Naples. The origin of this space is the 'Secret Museum' of erotic figures and sexually explicit inscriptions locked away in 1821 within the Museo Borbonico, where they were reserved only for gentlemen holding a special permission. It was made many times briefly accessible to the general public and then

Figure 4.2 Museum of Warsaw, Room of Architectural Details, a self-referential memento of the Lapidarium set up in the 1960s. The interpretive panel is signed by Ewa Perlińska-Kobierzyńska, curator of the room.

Source: Photo by J. Pedro Lorente, with kind permission from Muzeum Warszawy

closed again up to the end of the 1960s, before being definitively reopened in 2000. After so many refurbishments and changes in the contents, the present state of this space cannot be described as a reconstruction, but one cannot avoid a sense of the original voyeuristic experience looking at porn Pompeian frescoes and sculptures, closed behind an impressive gate which youngsters are still not allowed to cross unless accompanied by an adult. Another historic environment just apparently preserved for posterity in a museum, despite continuous changes, is the overall look of the Pitt Rivers Museum in Oxford University. Because of its crowded displays in dark-coated showcases housed within a typical cast-iron nineteenth-century architecture, most people think it is a fossilised Victorian museography and this is the deceiving 'first impression' intended by the staff. But the curators are scholars updated in the latest anthropological tendencies, thus they have modified many times the arrangement of displays, loosely keeping General Pitt Rivers' preference for typological groupings, which are now subranged according to thematic and geographical criteria. After the intense 2009 refurbishing, many more things have been altered in order to keep the look as if everything remains more or less the same. Similar criteria have guided the most recent museographical reconstitutions of the Teylers Museum in Haarlem, to enhance its identity as an 'authentic' legacy of the Enlightenment, even though it had undergone so many transformations over the centuries (Bouquet, 2012). Further examples can be located in France, where some institutions have decided to proudly reinforce attention to their 'historic' displays, as the curiosity cabinet of the Musée Joseph Denais in Beaufort-en-Vallée, revamped in 2011, or the former 1970s museography evoked at the Musée des Beaux-Arts de Besançon since 2018 after intense renovations.

Building on such precedents, it is not surprising to find nowadays shows tackling bogus remakes of historic avant-garde displays, like Malevich's *Last Futurist Exhibition* emulated in Máribor in 2008 (Hansen, 2011: 47) or László Moholy-Nagy's *Raum der Gegenwart*, El Lissitzky's *Abstraktes Kabinett* and Lina Bo Bardi's display for the Museu de Arte de São Paulo, all three re-staged in Einhoven in 2010/11 by means of conceptual installations, which were saluted as re-readings of art history paradigmatic of 'radical museology' (Bishop, 2014: 33). In fact, the MASP has then opted for a somehow scenographic recreation of the stunning modernist parade of its masterpieces devised by Lina Bo Bardi in the form of a forest of more than 100 glass and concrete easels, which had been removed during a 1996 refurbishment. It is more or less back in place again since 2015, with an information panel installed at the entrance by Bradesco, the bank company sponsoring this recreation, describing it as 'rescate preciso de uma peça icónica' [precise rescue of an iconic piece] even though the materials used look quite different, following professional restoration standards to make this intervention recognisable as new.

In general, the prevailing option is not to rebuild new architectural replicas of lost museographies, instead they are preferably evoked via mockups, virtual reality, photo montages or other educational documents that will not be perceived as deceiving reconstructions. Faithful to this didactic strategy, some reproductions on a small scale of historic exhibition displays of American modernity, mainly referring to the shows curated by Alfred Barr or Dorothy Miller for the MoMA in New York, are purposely displayed in the Museum of American Art in Berlin, opened in 2004 to explain this specific museographical topic. Very specialised as well is the erudite homage staged at the Moderna Museet in Stockholm, in a space reserved for the collection bequeathed by its most famous director Pontus Hultén, whose memory is honoured there by placing these artworks in a storing/display system that recalls the mechanic devices implemented by him when he was director of the Museum of Modern Art at the Pompidou Centre in Paris (Burch, 2012). More popular has become another metonymical restaging implemented in 2012 by the transfer of the Barnes Foundation from the founders' home in the suburbs of Merion to a new building in the centre of Philadelphia, after bitter judiciary conflicts. Although Albert Barnes had bequeathed his house and collection stating in his will that all his modern paintings should remain in exactly the same place, this has been freely interpreted as a reference not to the edifice but to the arrangements of pictures, which are hung again in roughly similar ensembles, recreated according to the collector's taste and ideas, which are described to visitors as forming part of Barnes' cultural legacy (Lawrence, 2015).

If former display systems are thus recognised as worthy heritage, complementary to the intrinsic value of their contents, it seems obvious that such curatorial legacies should also deserve to be self-referentially highlighted in museums and exhibitions. Paraphrasing Marshall McLuhan's famous dictum, we could state that for critical museologists the medium is now part of the message to be reflexively considered. Indeed, museums across the world are now proudly informing their visitors about, for example, the historic interest of their old dioramas, dating sometimes back to the early twentieth century. Some institutions are still pursuing the ambitious idea of replicating historic exhibitions; although this is almost an impossible task because, even if we could reunite again the same contents in the same space, conserved scrupulously unaltered, our present professional standards of public appreciation and safety have totally changed. This was a lesson learned in the first decade of the new millennium at Tate Modern and other museums where the tantalising challenge of re-doing legendary art shows has revealed as unattainable, though highly regarding for educational gains in critical self-reflection, as Helen Rees Leahy declared, in an essay suggestively entitled 'Making an Exhibition of Ourselves', pondering to what extend is an exhibition of an exhibition a (re)production or an exhibitionist display of institutional capacity for self-critique (Rees Leahy, 2012: 150). That should be the ultimate scientific goal in museums, unlike some popular versions of historic re-enactments which encourage celebrative engagement discouraging critical thinking (Watson, 2015: 290 and 296). In consequence, the history of museums and exhibitions is being scholarly revised from the standpoint of our present fascination with theatrical props and digital technologies (Sompairac, 2016).

It would perhaps be a logical corollary to complement original museographic heritage with interpretations in any kind of support, which should be problematised explanations – rather like a 'critical edition' of a reconstructed text comes with variants and remarks in footnotes. The Louvre is thus documenting *in situ*, by means of didactic room sheets and explanatory panels illustrated with ancient photos, the former display criteria of the *Salon Carré*, the *Grande Galerie* or other key areas of the museum, so as to make visitors aware of curatorial changes and continuities over time. An old white and black photography at the entrance to every room in the ground floor of the Victor Balaguer Museum in Vilanova i la Geltrú (Barcelona) shows how the same collection was arranged in the nineteenth century, which invites guests to sharpen eyes and mind spotting the differences and similarities. Another of my favourite examples of this sort of museographical visual thinking strategy was produced at the National Museum of Anthropology in Mexico City displaying a replica of Moctezuma's feather crown, as Vienna's Weltmuseum owns the original, whose demanded repatriation ignited for decades diplomatic tension with Austria: in 2010, I saw tourists smilingly taking photos of themselves standing in front of the replica, hung for this purpose in a showcase at head height; but next to it an enlarged historic black and white photo featured indigenous visitors of yore bent to look at that facsimile headdress in respectful reverence, prompted by its former installation in a lower show-window. In many other cases, the visual parallelism contrasting past and present is intended to convey feelings of progress, as in the Vatican Museum's collection of Etruscan antiques, where an explanatory panel in several languages includes a picture of how these bronzes and stones were overcrowding the room a century ago. Indeed, this visual collation recalls commercial advertisements juxtaposing two images of the same person before and after some remedial treatment; more unbiased would be a parallelism of three or more views, documenting diverse arrangements in different epochs, as the National Museum of Colombia has done in its 'sala de banderas' – main room – illustrating a large panel entitled '¿Qué se ha contado en esta sala?' [What has been told in this room?] (Lorente, 2014: 112 & 114).

By self-referentially retrieving former displays, museums are thus offering us a reflexion of themselves as narratives under permanent (re)construction. Confronted with historic museographies, visitors are sometimes provoked to espouse critical reviews from a new perspective. Sheila Watson put as an example the Museum of Political History in St Petersburg, founded in 1957 to glorify the Great October Socialist Revolution, exalted in painted murals and displays many of which have been safeguarded but radically reinterpreted with ironic comments (Watson, 2015: 292). What is ultimately exhibited is the museum itself and its history, making the public aware that what they see was previously shown in a similar way but telling something different. Museums recalling idiosyncratic presentations from other times today are not necessarily intending to cultivate nostalgia for the past but professionally keeping and interpreting museographical evidences for posterity. If the history of exhibitions and museums has become a cardinal feature in critical heritage studies, it must logically be a matter of interest for museums themselves.

4.2 Museums that show their own history: critical autobiographies?

As historical displays and the criteria implemented in their staging have encouraged in some museums critical (self-)reflection about their respective past, these types of reconsiderations would also find their place in the rooms allocated by museums to tell their own history as institutions. Often conceived as preliminary presentations, such introductory spaces had initially attached particular significance to the building construction and its makeovers. A perfectly reasonable order of priority, since the edifice is the first thing that visitors see, often in the form of an imposing architecture, particularly in cases of reconverted historical monuments whose vicissitudes well deserved some explanation for the benefit of the public. Introductory boards with texts and illustrative images would be displayed encapsulating a chronicle that could be expanded with the purchase of a booklet or guide in the museum shop, usually located by the entrance.

This well-known *modus operandi* reached momentum in 1989, when the Louvre inaugurated the new entrance below I.M. Pei's pyramid. In the access to the Sully wing, some freely accessible rooms didactically narrated the architectural evolution of the former castle and royal palace as well as the successive extensions of the museum in that monumental precinct. That historical preface caught the attention of some museumgoers with an interest in history or those who merely needed entertainment while waiting for relatives or friends. Most people, however, would simply peek in, dashing in the direction of the Mona Lisa or other gems in the museum's collection. Those rooms have been replaced with new spaces where the expanded historical account seems better integrated in the museum visit while the architectural-centred approach gives way to multifaceted perspectives about the past of such memorable institution. Yet, architecture continues to play a major part in historical preambles elsewhere: for instance, the ground floor of the Capodimonte Museum of Naples displaying between the entrance and the ticket offices several boards about the history of the palace and museum, which exclusively focus on the successive renovations up to the last one, finished by 1999.

With the passing of time and the development of new technologies, video displays and spectacular multimedia presentations are taking over. However, what remains largely unchanged is the celebrative historical approach of the standard welcoming exordium – usually outlining the museum's building process and its renovations/extensions, the relevance and expansion of its collections or other notable events. A quick and self-indulgent revision, which often zeroes in on the museum's foundational period, acts as a historical preface habitually sited off the museum's main route. It is now the case of the room with a striking introductory audiovisual in the Guggenheim Museum Bilbao: *Zero Espazioa*. It opened as an interactive educational prelude in 2010 being totally reformed in 2018 on the occasion of the twentieth anniversary of the institution. Located just before the box office, it allows tourists who choose not to purchase the pricy entrance ticket to enjoy the compelling audiovisual display that celebrates the 'Bilbao effect'. Whether they visit the exhibitions indoors or not, viewers will experience the epiphany of a world-famous 'miracle', still attracting thousands of cultural pilgrims. This museum undoubtedly has reasons to make people feel proud of its success, though the barrage of criticism and protests it has sparked are totally absent and they should also form part of its history. Similarly, the historical preamble set in 2019 at the new underground entrance to Berlin's Museumsinsel, called James-Simon Galerie, recounts the development of the entire museum complex from a reductionist point of view, according to Annette Loeseke. She would have preferred a 'transhistorical' reflection that should critically link the past and the present of each of the museums on the island (Loeseke, 2019: 148). All in all, it must be pointed out that besides the manifold didactic resources including models, projections and plasma screens, some showcases do display a selection of original emblematic pieces from the various museums. A remarkable effort, since resorting to authentic elements from the building and the collection as testimonies to its architectural and institutional history adds curatorial merit to the account. Instead of a merely textual or oral narration complemented by photographs or other illustrations, chosen items from the museum's collections thus serve to document its past and evolution.

Some museums are thus producing a more sophisticated autobiographical introduction, availing not only of educational accessories but also of some of their own catalogued collections. An outstanding instance is the so-called *Enlightenment Gallery*, inaugurated in 2003 on the occasion of the two-hundred-and-fiftieth anniversary of the British Museum: the former King's library, meticulously restored to its purported original design, no longer houses books – now kept in the new British Library – instead, its glass cabinets show a varied selection of representative objects, typical of refined eighteenth-century collecting, as an introduction to the museum's origin and cosmopolitan approach (Lord, 2005: 148–151). Pertinently, the main access is gained through the large central court covered with Norman Foster's glass and steel canopy. In this courtyard, we find the museum's largest shop with books and memorabilia to broaden information concerning this institution and to act as a historical 'starter' in this space – Room 1 in the museum map – from which to access Room 2, titled *Collecting the World*, with the Waddesdon Bequest of Renaissance and Baroque master-pieces from different countries on the one side and the stairs to the upper floor on the other. But the historical narration does not continue anywhere else on the tour through one of the world's oldest museums, which has elic-ited numerous and often controversial studies.

Architecture and collecting would remain in many cases the favourite lines of argument of a partially autobiographical review presented by most museums as a starting point, often almost exclusively focussed on celebrat-ing their foundational era. An exceptional deviation to this pattern is per-haps the judgemental presentation that the Museo Nacional de Costa Rica used to make of its building and institution in an initial section called *From Barracks to Museum*, located in the dungeons of the former military com-plex. Costa Ricans enjoy visiting the once fearsome Bellavista Barracks, precisely the place where the abolition of the army was signed, marking the start of a period of peace and prosperity, when this former centre of repression became the national museum. In 2008, the prisoners' lavatories and the graffiti in their cells were restored while maintaining the gilded cof-fered ceilings brought from the old Congress building and displaying pho-tographs of showcases with religious objects that used to be exhibited there. These striking visual contrasts propitiate viewing the old barracks as a hei-nous episode now fortunately over and provide a questioning outlook of the peculiar foundational museum setup; but such surreptitious criticism was somehow muffled by the forbearing tone of this prefatory exhibition, pur-portedly adopting a low profile in order not to offend viewers' sensibilities.

As a matter of fact, an explicitly revisionist discourse is rarely adopted in these opening rooms dedicated by museums to their foundational years. Even in cases where an episode in their early history may have been the subject of critical reconsideration, they frequently choose to overlook it or even condone it. A telling example can be found right at the entrance of the Ashmolean Museum of Oxford, in the introductory room that commemo-rates its origins. The museum has always boasted of being one of the oldest in the world, founded in 1682 when Elias Ashmole gifted his collection from the *Museum Tradescantianum* to the University. It made sense to allocate a particular space to such a foundational bequest in 2009 when the ambitious remodelling process was tackled. But only a succinct summary of the history of the museum from then on was provided, omitting the regrettable episode of the destruction of the Tradescant's dodo, still conserved by the eight-eenth century until a curator decided it was no longer worth showing and burnt it, keeping only its legs and head.[2] An incident now recalled, though very briefly, after the renovation of this introductory room since 2017 titled the *Ashmolean Story*. As in a tale, this attractive account mythologises the foundational collection rather than delivering a critical history of over three centuries of the museum's activity. Quite the opposite of the new underground gallery inaugurated at Tervuren Museum, reopened in 2018 as the Africa Museum, which welcomes visitors to a challenging reinterpretation of Belgian colonialism in its historical (self-)reflexion on the past, present and future of the institution.

However, leaving aside exceptional cases like that, such introductory spaces tend to be new instances of the traditional exaltation of the 'founding fathers' of each institution. An exemplary case may be found in the East Slovak Museum of Košice, reopened in 2013 after the renovation of its permanent exhibition, whereas no mention is made of heritage policies in communist Czechoslovakia, the introductory room is dedicated to collecting in the period of the founder, Imrich Henszlmann, with a commemorative installation of salvaged nineteenth-century showcases, recovered from the museum storerooms. In China, a combination of nostalgic pride in its origins and silence over later developments seems to have prevailed since 2018 in the final gallery of the Museum of Nanjing, one of the oldest in China, as it was established in 1933. Photographs and souvenirs explain the initial glory of the institution when the city was a thriving capital, until the Kuomintang government in 1949 transferred to Taiwan the best pieces in the collection, now housed in Taipei's National Palace Museum. Likewise, the underground floor of the Ethnological Museum of Barcelona pays tribute to its founder and first director, August Panyella i Gómez, to his collaborator and wife Zeferina Amil i Mengual and to other forerunners whose portraits and biographies feature in big panels, homaging only personalities of yore.

Nevertheless, other museums of anthropology have in recent times been reviewing those foundational figures, who are being critically evaluated from a post-colonial viewpoint based on activism in defence of racial equality. Controversies rarely go as far as in the case of Sir Baldwin Spencer in Australia, no longer revered by the Melbourne Museum. More nuanced is the reconsideration of Dr Pedro González Velasco and his Museo Velasco at the National Museum of Anthropology in Madrid. Since 1992 a room next to the entrance, called *Room of the origins of the museum*, had been dedicated to his legacy; but in 2015 the current director revisited such an approach and added explanatory boards written in Spanish and in English with photographs of the history of the museum including not always flattering remarks. A written comment contrasts the arrangement set by Dr Velasco on the wing of the museum dedicated to medicine with the 'lack of criterion' evinced in the part of the museum dealing with other curios because of the variegated array of specimens from various periods. Another explanatory board expounds with epistemological distancing the museum's development from an anatomical perception of anthropology to a cultural approach. For this reason, the skeleton of the giant man from Extremadura – the most popular attraction at the onset – is fittingly displayed in this quiet and more intimate room, as testimony to how much deontological criteria have changed over the years concerning the musealisation of human remains.

The success of this space set aside to reflect on some turning points in the history of a national museum and its own professional criteria inspired others in the rest of Spain, such as the Museum of León, with a section at the end of its permanent exhibition dedicated to the concept of heritage and to the history of the establishment since its reopening in 2007. Similarly, the Archaeological Museum of Asturias, after its renovation in 2011, reserved a room by landing of the stairs on the second floor to tell the development of archaeology in the region and the history of the institution in a display titled *From collection to Museum*, combining materials from excavations, photographs, old furniture pieces, a video, etc. However, these spaces of reflection about previous stages of curatorship usually remain well apart from the museum regular trail whether they are devised as an introduction or as the end of the visit or as both. For example, since 2015 Room A of the National Sculpture Museum of Valladolid presents the *Memory of the Museum* behind a solid wooden door that visitors need to open if so inclined to by their curiosity; though it is sometimes closed to the public when there is a shortage of security personnel. Thus, this part of the museum tour is too often short-circuited and ignored by visitors, failing to engage in the meta-discourse nowadays considered essential by critical museologists.

To be sure, sometimes the museum narrative confers special attention to such reflexive spaces encouraging curatorial and epistemological recon-siderations of past cultural policies. Particularly praiseworthy are the two self-referencing sections offered by the National Archaeological Museum of Madrid, reopened in 2014 with a totally renovated layout, which starts by the new entrance with an introduction hall explaining what Archaeol-ogy is – including presentations about the evolution of this discipline in Spain – and ends with the history of the museum in Room 31 of the top floor. Images and items presented there as historical documents review some major episodes in its development, starting with the origins of the museum, as pointed by the sign *From Cabinet to museum* displayed by the door; once inside, however, the welcoming notice appropriately reveals a broader scope: *Where our past lives: The National Archaeological Museum*. Indeed, a very complete and somehow critical autobiography is offered here, much to the enjoyment of many customers, who eagerly spend their time in this final section. Even more so in the case of the Museo del Prado after the inauguration in 2021 of a similar unit called 'Prado 200', which renders an overview of the museum's two-hundred years of history through sculptures, photographs, etchings, models, paintings, plans or other material from its archive and library installed in a spectacular basement. A punctilious reflection of the Prado's evolution, it is divided into successive time units covering a range of issues from its architecture or public image to its main exhibitions and activities.

This dual approach, combining the history of the building with that of the institution has originated two different sections in other cases. Most notably in Bogotá where the National Museum of Colombia, refurbished in 2020, proposes a diversion of narratives: on the one hand *Historia del Panóptico*, telling the history of the former prison prior to its present use, and on the other hand *La historia del museo y el museo en la historia*, reflecting in parallel storylines three historical stages in the development of this museum or other comparable institutions in the same country, in Latin America and in the world (Figure 4.3). But the separation is much more explicit at the Museo de Málaga since 2016, as the visit starts on the ground floor with the history of the building – originally a Customs Palace – then continues on the second floor with an evocation of the Museo Loringiano and the origins of the archaeological collection, whereas on the first floor the permanent display of fine arts is framed between a space devoted to the museum founded in the nineteenth century by the Academy of San Telmo and a final

Figure 4.3 Gallery about the history of the museum at the *Museo Nacional de Colombia*, Bogotá.

Source: Photo by Sandra Vargas, Museo Nacional de Colombia

room entitled *Un museo cargado de historia* [A museum steeped in history].
Moreover, this complex history is not only explained in specific sections,
as its most important protagonists are recalled throughout the museum on
special labels containing a brief biography and a summary of their relationship with the institution. This, according to Prof. Isabel García Fernández,
constitutes a trait of twenty-first century museography (García Fernández,
2019: 26–27). She considers that museums strive to become more human,
unfolding their stories in the form of personal accounts.

Indeed, this strategy of splitting up the autobiography of the museum
all over the building might have been inspired by the Parisian *Musée de
l'Homme*, reopened in 2015 after years of refurbishment work. The trail called
Histoire(s) du Musée de l'Homme goes from the ground floor of the Palais de
Chaillot up to the library on the top floor, with tributes to some members of
the staff who participated in the Resistance, a showcase on the second floor
and, above all, two massive displays in the lobby of the first floor narrating
on one side the architectural developments and on the other summarising the
history of the institution and of the former Musée d'Ethnographie. Particular
emphasis is paid to the prestigious nineteenth- and twentieth-century experts
attached to this museum, including the celebrated museologist George-Henri
Rivière and, of course, the museum's founder, ethnologist Paul Rivet, after
whom the great *Atrium* is named (Figure 4.1). Thus, either before accessing
the permanent exhibition rooms or when climbing the stairs, one inevitably stumbles across these episodes of vast historical reflection availing of
a variety of 'museum materials': statues and busts, old signage and labels,
postcards, etc.

Specific signage and explanatory labels punctuating with historical souvenirs successive stages of the museum visit can thus activate a continuous reflexive correlation of past and present. Sometimes by using memorial
plaques, like those we see on the façades when walking down the street, in
memory of a certain event or character, such as the one placed in front of the
entrance to the assembly hall of the Art Institute of Chicago, in memory of the
famous speech pro religious tolerance delivered there by Swami Vivekananda
on September 11, 1893. Another museum that for years has multiplied the
points of parallel interconnection between the presentation of its collections
and its own history is the Louvre. Information posters concerning the *Histoire du Palais* are colour-coded and placed preferentially on access walls
between rooms or in some hidden corners so that the particulars about what
was on display at the *Salon Carré* or about the ceiling decoration in the *Musée
Charles X* or other historical details do not outshine the museum's collection
on display. Especially noteworthy is the *Pavillon de l'Horloge*, devoted since
2016 to narrating the Louvre's complex history. It begins on the ground floor
with the medieval fortress by the Seine erected in the twelfth century and

other constructions added during its time as a museum. It then continues on the second floor with the history of the collections and of the most relevant individuals involved in their acquisition, curatorship and reorganisation and ends on the third floor with current interventions, the latest restorations, excavations and social actions, the new museum branch in Lens and, of course, the Louvre Abu Dhabi, the Emirate that paid for all these new rooms dedicated to the history of the Louvre. For this reason, its official name is the 'Sheik Zayed Bin Sultan Al Nahyan Interpretation Centre'.

Obviously, no reference is made to the controversies and criticisms harvested by the bombastic satellite museum on Saadiyat Island. The historical review is overall laudatory and even the ascending trail to the top floor seems to be at the service of the glorifying apotheosis that crowns it. Not precisely a paradigm of critical autobiography, this Louvre section constitutes, however, an excellent self-referencing museographic model. Firstly, because museum personnel acquire huge relevance in the narration – the second floor focuses on some directors and curators – showing that the history of the Louvre Museum not only concerns the building and its collections but also the work of its staff. Secondly, unlike other museums where spaces dedicated to their own history are given rather secondary or marginal value, this pavilion is a 'must see' for visitors to the Louvre displaying its prestigious history with abundant original materials including models, plans, statues and paintings, some extremely valuable. Another estimable feature of this autobiographic chronicle is that all museum trails throughout the Louvre seem to merge at the *Pavillon de l'Horloge*, linked to the other rooms on each of the floors through multiple curatorial and architectural interconnecting junctions. Far from being a cul-de-sac or a complement to the museum visit, each episode in this historical narrative is intelligently interconnected to the surrounding sections of the museum. The history of the building begins on the underground level next to the moat of the medieval palace and some archaeological finds, then the part titled 'One museum, many collections' is on the first floor amidst ancient Greco-Roman pieces and the collections of decorative arts, whereas on the second floor, in the middle of a circuit entirely dedicated to French painting, the present and future of the country's most prestigious cultural institution is narrated as part of such patriotic narrative. One can therefore make one's way up through the pavilion following the order of the historical account or encounter it as one visits the different parts of the Louvre.

This constitutes an exceptional instance, since very few museums worldwide have so much to tell about their evolution either in terms of architecture or as institutions. Yet an increasing number of them opt to allocate an area of historical self-reflection appropriately interconnected with their museographical trail. In Boston, the Museum of Fine Arts, which was expanded and fully refurbished in 2010, displays on the curved walls around the stairs of the section on European art, just above the Sharf Visitor Center, a space for remembrance with photographs, documents and pieces from the collection including some paintings of iconographic value such as Enrico Meneghelli's renowned *The Lawrence Room, Museum of Fine Arts Boston*. Quite remarkably, this autobiographical exploration titled *Preserving History, Making History: The Museum of Fine Arts, Boston* reviews the museum from its origins until its recent expansion and even its future plans – or the other way around, depending on where the visit starts. If only more museums would accompany reflections about their past with testimonies about present debates and future challenges! (Fábrega García, 2020: 26).

Unfortunately, this type of museological argument cannot always be communicated but through the use of words – complemented with charts, images or other materials. The same applies to facts about the progress of the activities carried out by the respective departments of education, security, public relations, etc. Original alternatives do exist. For instance, the MuHKA of Antwerp covered the wall that connects all the floors in the building with posters of the main temporary exhibitions displayed since the inauguration of the current building. Or the anniversaries of events that museums share on social networks that on such day this or that happened: an autobiography of sorts administered in small doses to present themselves to society. Indeed, the most appropriate means for museums to tell their story continue to be books, whose presence in the museum shops is decreasing in favour of souvenirs and merchandising. Perhaps it would be a good idea to provide books freely for reference in the areas dedicated to reflecting on the history of the institution, just as catalogues or complementary bibliographies are often available on tables or lecterns for curious visitors to expand their knowledge of the topic of temporary exhibitions. This would contribute to opening up new horizons to critical museology inasmuch as some of those books about the museum would be written by authors from both within and outside the corresponding institution, possibly even holding critical opinions of it.

Notes

1 In particular, the *Kabinett der Abstrakten*, created by El Lissitzky on the second floor of Hannover Landesmuseum followed by László Moholy-Nagy's *Raum der Gegenwart* to conclude the art historical itinerary arranged by director Alexander Dorner: that famous cabinet of abstract artworks had been dismantled by the Nazis in 1937 and remade from scratch in 1968 at the heart of the then renamed Niedersächsischen Landesmuseum in Room 45 of the ground floor: a displacement further stressed by its transfer in 1979 to the new building of the Sprengel

Museum, where renewed replicas were re-elaborated in 1983 and 2017 (Tejeda Martín, 2012).

2 The dodo is an extinct species of bird native to the island of Mauritius that became an Oxonian icon because of its leading role in *Alice in Wonderland*. Its image presides over Room 2 of the Ashmolean as a hidden message to the initiated because any Museology student is familiar with the episode of the destruction of the only remaining specimen, usually quoted as an instance of an unfortunate curatorial decision. Instead, however, that incident seems to be justified by the museum: 'the Tradescant's famous dodo was in such an advanced state of decay it was considered beyond redemption and removed from display (today the head and one foot survive in the University Museum of Natural History)'. www.ashmolean.org/history-ashmolean (retrieved on 30th September 2021)

5   Final considerations

The argumentative logic of this book moves from the general to the specific, and from museum theory to praxis while advocating personal critical reflection. So, finally, it seems appropriate to end it with some insights into what I have bypassed. For example, my reluctance in Chapter 1 to formulate definitions of 'critical museology' might seem shocking. Especially considering the present intensity of terminological debates, even regarding the very concept of 'museum', although we have hardly advanced in this issue. Perhaps critical museology reached the climax of its worldwide influence in September 2019 when the proposal for a change in the museum notion was presented for approval by the General Assembly of ICOM in Kyoto:

> Museums are democratising, inclusive and polyphonic spaces for critical dialogue about the pasts and the futures. Acknowledging and addressing the conflicts and challenges of the present, they hold artefacts and specimens in trust for society, safeguard diverse memories for future generations and guarantee equal rights and equal access to heritage for all people.
> Museums are not for profit. They are participatory and transparent, and work in active partnership with and for diverse communities to collect, preserve, research, interpret, exhibit, and enhance understandings of the world, aiming to contribute to human dignity and social justice, global equality and planetary wellbeing.

After heated debate and an overwhelming majority of votes against, the proposal was rejected. I must admit I also did not quite like this long and abstruse definition, in which many key concepts from recent museological literature had been included, but a crucial term such as 'education' was missing. Since then, efforts to agree on definitions have been redoubled everywhere, although I very much doubt that a terminological agreement will

DOI: 10.4324/9781003263050-6

Figure 5.1 Lettering on the façade of the Museum of Memory and Human Rights in Santiago de Chile.

Source: Photo by J. Pedro Lorente

be reached by critical museologists: if something characterises us is above all the defence of personal criteria and dissent. Thus, it would be almost an incongruence to claim a normative definition of 'critical museology'! True enough, I wrote a synthetic characterisation of 'critical museology/ muséologie critique' in the bilingual *Dictionary of Museology/Dictionnaire de Muséologie* which, under the editorial coordination of Prof. François Mairesse, will soon be published by ICOM; however, each entry in that dictionary is signed by its respective author and does not necessarily respond to unanimously assumed definitions.[1]

Nor is there any agreement when it comes to identifying critical museology with a specific type of institution, the epitome of which could be a certain museum of anthropology, or of contemporary art, or of historical/political memory. Some of them have been mentioned in these pages as exemplary cases for one aspect or another, but none 100% fit neither this label nor other relatable terms, such as the 'interrogative museum', 'participatory museum', 'mindful museum' or the 'disobedient museum', a designation proposed by Kylie Message in the inaugural volume of the book series 'Museums in Focus' to allude to non-institutional experiences of a critical nature in a conceptual border-space among the museum, the intellectual sphere and the street (Message, 2018: 84). I am fascinated by these interspatial and transdisciplinary boundaries, particularly the study of museums in/as a public space, but I have not yet found a real example that seems conclusive to me. After Krzysztof Wodiczko's interventions on public monuments, onto which he projected poignant critical images, many other socially committed artists have also used museum façades as an interface; for example, members of the New York art collective The Illuminator, who aim to 'enlighten' fellow citizens on problematic issues using projections. In 2015, they placed messages about AIDS on the façades of hospitals but also on those of art museums, such as the Metropolitan or Guggenheim which, due to its iconic silhouette, is one of their favourite 'displaying supports'.

Artist and educator Luis Camnitzer also chose its curved walls facing the Fifth Avenue in New York as one of the destinations for his famous motto 'THE MUSEUM IS A SCHOOL:/THE ARTISTS LEARNS TO COMMUNICATE;/THE PUBLIC LEARNS TO MAKE CONNECTIONS'. Camnitzer's dictum has been displayed on the façades of museums in several countries in their respective languages, for example, it is permanently installed on the façade of the Museo de la Memoria y de los Derechos Humanos in Santiago de Chile (Figure 5.1). Not by chance, as the MMDH is often widely celebrated as a paradigm of critical museology. Yet when I visited it in 2014, the significance of the inscription went unnoticed to me for lack of information *in situ*, as I was not even able to recognise it as an artistic intervention or that its author was Camnitzer. Four years later, I could learn everything about it as a result of the great retrospective that the Museo Nacional Centro de Arte Reina Sofía dedicated to him in Madrid. So far, as noted in Chapter 2, the MNCARS does something similar with the works of Rogelio López Cuenca installed in front of its entrance; fortunately, however, both this and most other museums, either of arts or sciences, tend to extend their curatorial interpretation work to their collection pieces located outdoors. Now my main reproach is that sometimes one has the feeling that many institutions feel reassured just by placing – inside or outside the building – art interventions of 'institutional critique', even if their reflections do not penetrate the institutional discourse itself, which should involve visitors paying attention to controversies in museum work and their dilemmas (Lorente, 2013). Lately, Camnizer's motto has raised some objections and there are even those who suspect that this caption is serving museums as a declared legitimisation of their practices rather than as an internally assumed self-questioning challenge (Hoff, 2019: 311). This is a line of work that I have only outlined here to be developed in the future.

I am also expanding in other publications the comments condensed in Chapter 3 on the transition from the white cube to other museum architectures that enjoy less constrained viewing protocols as there are more and more windows or balconies that invite the crossing of gazes between interior and exterior to favour all kinds of cultural interrelations between the museum space and social life. From my own experience as a visitor and from other people's information, I am collecting many more examples of the empowerment of subjectivity in museums, but I am beginning to feel concerned about the dangers of going too far in this endeavour to enhance transparency and the human factor in institutions, when some persons at work are exhibited as visual lures. For many years now, it has been commonplace to let the public see a restaurateur in full swing, a trend that has spread to other staff members, in principle with a laudable intention, which is to make their job, and even their professional existence, more visible. But when seeing them on the other side of a glass or a barrier, sometimes there is a sad parallelism with animals in a zoo. Won't their mental focus and self-esteem suffer? I get uninhibited speaking in public because I enjoy establishing eye contact with the audience while I teach using a Power-Point; I have even argued oftentimes that this has been a suitable novelty at the service of 'critical history of art' compared to the traditional class with slides, when the students listened to the lecturer like an oracle emitting his/her voice in the dark behind the slide projector. However, I also need privacy to prepare my lessons or to write, and in the same way, for citizens to become aware of the curatorial work, it is not necessary to expose it all the time to the voyeuristic consumption of the masses. Meanwhile, a similar exhibitionism characterises the latest rituals of cultural consumers, taking selfies non-stop in front of iconic museum buildings and collections. Much has already been written about this practice, with some experts for and others against it, but discussion should be better redirected, according to the postulates of critical museology, so as to focus on the new ways of articulated interrelation. For example, praise should be given to initiatives such as 'Ask a Curator', which has made question-and-answer exchanges with heritage managers a global trending topic on Twitter.

Likewise, such technical resources are an excellent means to remind the public of the museum's historical events or past images of its history. This is especially true if communication does not work exclusively from the inside out, but also, on the contrary, when blogs and social networks encourage all sorts of audiences to participate not just as virtual consumers, but also as active generators of interpretations and suggestions. Rarely does this happen in the examples mentioned here in both the first part of Chapter 4, on the (re)presentation of historical museographies, or in the second part, on museum spaces dedicated to remembering their own history. An exceptional example has been successfully set by the American Museum of Natural History in New York: the decision not to cover or destroy a politically incorrect historic diorama, but to stick on the glass self-critical comments inviting people to ascertain 'why did we feel the need to update it?' could had been noticed by just some inquisitive visitors, yet it went viral through the museum website and social networks.[2] Furthermore, an article in *The New York Times* made it world news (Fota, 2019), which shows that art critics and cultural journalists could be excellent allies in this quest for public visibility/ reflexivity of museum curatorship.

Indeed, presumably, the greatest future challenge will lie in involving contemporary society in reframing historic heritage, that is, what Annette Loeseke calls 'Transhistoricism' saying:

> we need to contextualise and present as non-finite its institutional impact and shifting, ambiguous relation to power. Museums need to transparently communicate that they are contemporary as much as historical institutions; that they are about the present as much as the past.
>
> (Loeseke, 2019: 149)

This thought could also be applied to all *souvenirs* of the history of our museums and of museology as well since what we remember is always an expression of contemporary culture; even with historical museographies that are jealously kept as they were or of reflections written by past museologists. To pretend the opposite would be to indulge in naive 'allochronism', one of the errors denounced by critical anthropologist Fernando Estévez in his posthumous book entitled *Museopatías*, whose foreword, written by Anthony Shelton, pays tribute to that dear professor and activist by evoking some of his favourite topics – such as heritage, identity, tourism, souvenirs, or nostalgia – and by praising how he 'contributed enormously towards a critical museology whose essential vitality comes from the interaction of theory and practice' (in Estévez, 2019: 212). I make those words my own in the hope that this book will be another link in the chain to promote critical reflection that must flourish both inside and outside museums.

Notes

1 Here is the definition I wrote for the forthcoming dictionary of Museology (see also there the entry 'reflexive museology' signed by Bruno Brulon and Sharon Macdonald):

> Critical museology, also called 'reflexive museology', is a trend in museum studies developed in syntonic relation with the 'critical turn' instilled around the millennium change in cognate disciplines: e.g. 'critical pedagogy', 'critical sociology', 'critical anthropology', 'critical art history', etc.
>
> Taking the cue from the so-called "new museology", which contested institutional officialdom preaching social engagement and community empowerment, this critical reformulation has focused on the representation of minorities or peripheral cultures, the reconsideration from postcolonial

perspectives of ethical dilemmas about the exhibition and return of indigenous materials, the impugnation of dominant narratives, etc. Instead of celebratory discourses, a critical stance favours interrogations, dialectic counterpoints, plural stories and self-referential reflexivity, both in museum practice and in museological thinking.

2 American Museum of Natural History: Old New York Diorama www.amnh.org/exhibitions/permanent/theodore-roosevelt-memorial/hall/old-new-york-diorama (recovered on 20 October 2021)

References

Aidar, Gabriela (2020): "¿Es posible pensar en prácticas museológicas sociales y críticas dentro de los museos tradicionales?" In Giraud, Yves & Orellana Rivera, Isabel (coords.), *Actas. Coloquio Internacional de Museología Social, Participativa y Crítica*. Santiago de Chile: Ediciones Museo de la Educación Gabriela Mistral, pp. 301–310.

Alderton, Zoe (2014): "The secular sacred gallery: Religion at Te Papa Tongarewa", In Hartney, Christopher (ed.), *Secularisation: New Historical Perspectives*. Newcastle: Cambridge Scholars Publishing, pp. 251–272.

Alegría Licuime, Luis (2013): "Saber museológico y pensamiento crítico. ¿El giro subalterno?" *Cuadernos de Trabajo Educativos*, VII, pp. 4–12.

Alpers, Svetlana (1991): "The museum as a way of seeing", In Karp, Ivan & D. Lavine, Steven (eds.), *The Poetics and Politics of Museum Display*. Washington, DC-London: Smithsonian Institution Press, pp. 25–32.

Ames, Michael (1990): "Cultural empowerment and museums: Opening up anthropology through collaboration", In Pearce, Susan (ed.), *Objects of Knowledge*. London-Atlantic Highlands: The Athlone Press, pp. 158–173.

Ames, Michael (2006): "Counterfeit museology", *Museum Management and Curatorship* (21), pp. 171–186.

Ananiev, Vitaly (2013): *История зарубежной музеологии* (History of foreign museology). St. Petersburg: University of St. Petersburg.

Ang, Ien (2015): "Change and continuity. Art museums and the reproduction of art-museumness", In Witcomb, Andrea & Message, Kylie (eds.), *The International Handbooks of Museum Studies: Museum Theory*. Chichester: Wiley/Blackwell, pp. 211–231.

Araoz, Gustavo F. (2011): "Preserving heritage places under a new paradigm", *Journal of Cultural Heritage Management and Sustainable Development*, 1 (1), pp. 55–60.

Arias Serrano, Laura (2015): "Nuevos planteamientos museográficos en los museos de arte contemporáneo: de las primeras críticas al museo en los albores del siglo XX a los actuales microrrelatos", *Complutum*, 26 (2), pp. 133–143.

Arriaga, Amaia (2010): "Principios y estrategias de comunicación en las galerías Tate. Construyendo conocimiento sobre el arte", *AACA Digital* (11), junio 2010. www.aacadigital.com/contenido.php?idarticulo=325.

Arriaga, Amaia & Aguirre, Imanol (2020): "Museum-university collaboration to renew mediation in art and historical heritage. The case of the Museo de Navarra", *Arte, Individuo y Sociedad*, 32 (4), pp. 989–1008.

Ayala Aizpuro, Íñigo, Cuenca-Amigo, Macarena & Cuenca-Amigo, Jaime (2019): "Principales retos de los museos de arte en España. Consideraciones desde la museología crítica y el desarrollo de audiencias", *Aposta, Revista de Ciencias Sociales* (80), pp. 61–81.

Bal, Mieke (1992): "Telling, showing, showing off", *Critical Inquiry*, 18 (3), pp. 556–594.

Bal, Mieke (1996): "The discourse of the museum", In Greenberg, Reesa, Ferguson, Bruce W. & Nairne, Sandy (eds.), *Thinking About Exhibitions*. London-New York: Routledge, pp. 201–218.

Barrett, Jennifer (2011): *The Museum and the Public Sphere*. Hoboken, NJ: John Willey and Sons.

Barrett, Jennifer (2015): "Museums, human rights, and universalism reconsidered", In Wicomb, Andrea & Message, Kylie (eds.), *The International Handbooks of Museum Studies: Museum Theory*. New York: John Wiley & Sons, pp. 93–115.

Basu, Paul (2007): "The labyrinthine aesthetic in contemporary museum design", In MacDonald, Sharon & Basu, Paul (eds.), *Exhibition Experiments*. Oxford: Blackwell Publishers, pp. 47–70.

Bawin, Julie (2014): *L'artiste commissaire, entre posture critique, jeu créatif et valeur ajoutée*. Paris: Éditions des archives contemporaines.

Belda Navarro, Cristóbal & Marín Torres, María Teresa (eds.) (2004): *La Museología y la Historia del Arte*. Murcia: Universidad de Murcia-Fundación CajaMurcia.

Bernier, Christine (2002): *L'art au musée. De l'oeuvre à l'institution*. Paris-Budapest-Turin: L'Harmattan.

Beuvier, Franck (2003): "Une muséologie critique des objets exotiques: Autour de l'exposition 'Le musée cannibale'", *Gradhiva: revue d'histoire et d'archives de l'anthropologie*, pp. 119–124.

Bishop, Claire (2013): *Radical Museology, or, what's "contemporary" in museums of contemporary art?* London: Koening Books.

Bodenstein, Felicity & Pagani, Camilla (2014): "Decolonising national museums of ethnography in Europe: Exposing and reshaping colonial heritage (2000–2012)", In Chambers, Ian, et al. (eds.), *The Postcolonial Museum: The Arts of Memory and the Pressures of History*. Farnham-Burlington: Ashgate.

Borja-Villel, Manuel (2010): "¿Pueden los museos ser críticos? *Carta: Revista de pensamiento y debate del Museo Nacional Centro de Arte Reina Sofía*, 1, pp. 1–2.

Bouquet, Mary (2012): *Museums: A Visual Anthropology*. New York: Berg.

Boyd, Willard L. (1999): "Museums as centers of controversy", *Daedalus*, 128 (3), pp. 185–228.

Bronson, A. A. & Gale, P. (1983): *Museums by Artists*. Toronto: Art Metropole.

Brown, Claudine K. (2004): "The museum's role in a multicultural society", In Anderson, Gail (ed.), *Reinventing the Museum. Historical and Contemporary Perspectives on the Paradigm Shift*. Walnut Creek, CA-Oxford: Altamira Press, pp. 143–149.

Brulon Soares, Bruno (2015): "The museum performance. Reflecting on a Reflexive Museology", *Complutum*, 26 (2), pp. 49–57.

Brulon Soares, Bruno (2017): "A Museologia Reflexiva: recompondo os funda-
mentos de uma ciência contemporânea", In Brulon Soares, Bruno & Bernardo
Baraçal, Anaildo (eds.), *Stránský: uma ponte Brno – Brasil*. París-Rio de Janeiro:
ICOFOM-UNIRIO, pp. 144–160.

Brulon Soares, Bruno (2018): "Transculturación del conocimiento museológico",
Cuadernos Hispanoamericanos, 814, pp. 56–71.

Burch, Stuart (2012): "Past Presents and Present Futures: Rethinking Sweden's
Moderna Museet", *Future Anterior: Journal of Historic Preservation, History,
Theory, and Criticism*, 9 (2), pp. 97–111.

Butler, Shelley Ruth (2000): "The politics of exhibiting culture: Legacies and pos-
sibilities", *Museum Anthropology*, 23 (3), pp. 74–92.

Butler, Shelley Ruth (2013): "Reflexive Museology: Lost and Found", In Witcomb,
Andrea & Message, Kylie (eds.), *The International Handbooks of Museum Studies: Museum Theory*. New York: John Wiley & Sons, pp. 159–182.

Cameron, Duncan F. (1971): "The museum, a temple or the forum?" *Curator*, 14
(1), pp. 11–24.

Cameron, Duncan F. (1995): "The pilgrim and the shrine. The icon and the oracle.
A perspective on museology for tomorrow", *Museum Management and Curatorship*, 14 (1), pp. 48–57.

Carrier, David (2006): *Museum Skepticism: A History of the Display of Art in Public
Galleries*. Durham-London: Duke University Press.

Casey, Dawn (2001): "Museums as agents for social and political change", *Curator*,
44 (3), pp. 230–236.

Celis, Fernanda (2017): "L'ethnologie dans les musées d'ethnographie: déconnexions
et reconnexions disciplinaires", *Thesis. Cahiers d'Histoire des Collections et de
Muséologie* (17), pp. 33–49.

Chamberlain, Gregory (ed.) (2011): *The Radical Museum: Democracy, Dialogue
and Debate*. Stony Stratford, UK: Museum Identity Ltd.

Chambers, Marlene (2009): "Sometimes more is too much", *Curator*, 52 (1),
pp. 67–76.

Chiodi, Stefano (ed.) (2009): *Le funzioni del museo. Arte, museo, pubblico nella
contemporaneità*. Florence: Le Lettere.

Clifford, James (1997): *Routes: Travel and Translation in the Late Twentieth Century*. Cambridge, MA: Harvard University Press.

Clifford, James (2007): "Quai Branly in process", *October*, 120 (Spring), pp. 3–23.

Clifford, Timothy (1982): "The historical approach to the display of paintings", *International Journal of Museum Management and Curatorship* (1),
pp. 93–106.

Combariza, Marta, López Rosas, William Alfonso & Castell, Edmon (2014): *Museos
y museologías en Colombia. Retos y perspectivas*. Bogotá: Universidad Nacional
de Colombia, Maestría en Museología y Gestión del Patrimonio.

Conn, Steven (2010): *Do Museums Still Need Objects?* Philadelphia: University of
Philadelphia Press.

Corrin, Lisa G. (1994): "Mining the museum. Artists look at museums, museums
look at themselves", In Corrin, Lisa G. (ed.), *Mining the Museum: An Installation
by Fred Wilson*. New York: The New Press, pp. 1–22.

Crane, Susan A. (1997): "Memory, distortion and history in the museum", *History and Theory*, 36 (4), pp. 44–63.

Crenn, Gaëlle (2016): "La réforme muséale à l'heure postcoloniale. Stratégies muséographiques et reformulation du discours au Musée royal d'Afrique centrale (2005–2012)", *Culture & Musées*, 28, pp. 177–201.

Davallon, Jean (1992): "Le musée est-il vraiment un media?" *Public et musées* (2), pp. 99–123.

Davidson, Lee (2015): "Visitor studies: Toward a culture of reflective practice and critical museology for the visitor-centered museum", In McCarthy, Conal (ed.), *The International Handbooks of Museum Studies: Vol. 2 Museum Practice*. New York: John Wiley & Sons, pp. 503–527.

Davis, Douglas (1990): *The Museum Transformed. Design and Architecture in the Post-Pompidou Age*. New York: Abbeville Press.

Davis, Peter (1999): *Ecomuseums, a Sense of Place*. London-New York: Leicester University Press.

De Angelis, Alessandra, et al. (eds.) (2014): *The Postcolonial museum: The Arts of Memory and the Pressures of History*. Farnham-Burlington: Ashgate Publishing.

De Varine, Hugues (2017). *L'écomusée singulier et pluriel. Un témoignage sur cinquante ans de muséologie commuautaire dans le monde*. Paris: L'Harmattan.

Desvallées, André (ed.) (1992–93): *Vagues: une anthologie de la nouvelle muséologie*. Paris: Édition W.M.N.E.S., 2 vols.

Desvallées, André & Mairesse, François (eds.) (2010): *Key Concept of Museology*. Paris: Armand Colin-ICOM.

Desvallées, André & Nash, Suzanne (eds.) (2011): *The dialogic museum and the visitor experience./Le musée dialogique et l'expérience du visiteur./El museo dialógico y la experiencia del visitante*. Taipei-Paris: Council for Cultural Affairs of Taiwan-International Commitee for Museology, ICOM.

Dewdney, Andrew, Dibosa, David & Walsh, Victoria (2013): *Post-Critical Museology: Theory and Practice in the Art Museum*. London-New York: Routledge.

Dolák, Jan (2016): "Kritika kritické muzeologie", *Muzeológia a kultúrne dedičstvo*, 4 (2), pp. 21–33.

Donnellan, Caroline (2018): *Towards Tate Britain. Public Policy, Private Vision*. Abingdon-New York: Routledge.

Drouguet, Noémie (2007): "Quand l'artiste contemporain joue au muséographe", *CeROArt*, 1, pp. 1–17.

Duncan, Carol (1995): *Civilizing Rituals Inside Public Art Museums*. London: Routledge.

Duncan, Carol & Wallach, Allan (1978): "The museum of modern art as late capitalist ritual: An iconographic analysis", *Marxist Perspectives*, 1 (4), pp. 28–51 (edición revisada de un artículo previamente aparecido en el n° 194 de *Studio International*).

Duncan, Sally Anne (2002): "From period rooms to public trust: The authority debate and art museum leadership in America", *Curator*, 45 (2), pp. 93–108.

Elkins, James (1997): *Our Beautiful, Dry and Distant Texts*. London-New York: Routledge.

Estévez, Fernando (2019): *Museopatías*. Lanzarote: Fundación César Manrique.

Fábrega García, Tania (2020): "El museo, la primera obra. Formas de exponer la historia en los museos", In Baião, Joana & Matos, Lúcia Almeida (coords.), *Estraté-gias de exposição – História e práticas recentes*. Lisboa: Instituto de História da Arte-UNL, pp. 13–27.

Fehr, Michael (2000): "A museum and its memory. The art of recovering History", In Crane, Susan (ed.), *Museums and Memory*. Stanford: Stanford University Press, pp. 35–95.

Fernández, Olga & Río, Víctor del (eds.) (2007): *Estrategias críticas para una práctica educativa en el arte contemporáneo*. Valladolid: Fundación Patio Herreriano.

Fernández López, Olga (2020): *Exposiciones y comisariado. Relatos cruzados*. Madrid: Cátedra.

Flórez Crespo, María del Mar (2006): "La museología crítica y los estudios de público en los museos de arte contemporáneo: caso del Museo de Arte Contemporáneo de Castilla y León (MUSAC)", *De arte: revista de historia del arte* (Univ. de León) (5), pp. 231–243.

Fota, Ana (2019): "What's wrong with this diorama? You can read all about it?" *The New York Times*, March 21, 2019, section C, page 1. www.nytimes. com/2019/03/20/arts/design/natural-history-museum-diorama.html.

Fraser, Andrea (2005): "From the critique of institutions to an institution of critique", *Artforum*, 44 (1), pp. 278–283.

García Canclini, Néstor (2010): "¿Los arquitectos y el espectáculo les hacen mal a los museos?" In Castilla, Américo (comp.), *El museo en escena. Política y cultura en América Latina*. Buenos Aires: Paidós, pp. 131–144.

García Fernández, Isabel (2015): "El papel de los museos en la sociedad actual: discurso institucional o museo participativo", *Complutum*, 26 (2), pp. 39–47.

García Fernández, Isabel (2019): "La nueva museografía", *Revista de Museología*, 75, pp. 21–33.

Geismar, Haidy (2015): "The art of anthropology. Questioning contemporary art in ethnographic display", In Witcomb, Andrea & Message, Kylie (eds.), *The International Handbooks of Museum Studies: Museum Theory*. New York: John Wiley & Sons, pp. 183–210.

Giebelhausen, Michaela (ed.) (2003): *The Architecture of the Museum: Symbolic Structures, Urban Contexts*. Manchester: Manchester University Press.

Gob, André (2010): *Le musée, une institution dépassée?* Paris: Armand Colin.

Gob, André & Drouguet, Noémie (2010): *La muséologie: Histoire, développements, enjeux actuels*. Paris: Armand Colin (third edition).

Gómez Martínez, Javier (2006): *Dos museologías. Las tradiciones anglosajona y mediterránea: diferencias y contactos*. Gijón: Trea.

Gómez Martínez, Javier (2011): "Estrategias de museografía crítica para romper las barreras con el público", *Museo y Territorio*, 4, pp. 133–141.

Gómez Martínez, J. (2016): *Museografía al filo del milenio. Tendencias y recurrencias*. Gijón: Trea.

Gonseth, Marc-Olivier (2013): "Ethnographic data and expographic process: A need for interpretative theories, (micro-) fieldworks, transverse analyses and poetic irony", In Ferracutti, Sandra (ed.), *Beyond Modernity: Do Ethnography Museums need Ethnography?* Rome: Espera Libreria Archeologica.

Graham, Janna, Graziano, Valeria & Kelly, Susan (2016): "The educational turn in art: Rewriting the hidden curriculum", *Performance Research*, 21 (6), pp. 29–35.

Grau Lobo, Luis A. (2010): "Nueva Museología versus Museología Crítica: En busca de un patrón perdido", En *Actas de los XX Cursos Monográficos sobre el Patrimonio Histórico:[Reinosa, julio de 2009]*. Santander: Servicio de Publicaciones de la Universidad de Cantabria, pp. 305–316.

Grau Lobo, Luis A. (2020): *El cristal y las sombras. Sobre museos y otras ilusiones*. León, Domus Pucelae y menoslobos.

Green, Alison (2018): *When Artists Curate. Contemporary Art and the Exhibition as Medium*. London: Reaktion Books.

Grinell, Klas & Gustavsson Renius, Lotten (2013): "The king is dead. Long live the king! Un-inheriting modern ethnography while inheriting objects of ethnography", In Ferracuti, Sandra & Frasca, Elisabetta (eds.), *Beyond Modernity: Do Ethnographic Museums Need Ethnography?* Rome: Espera.

Gurian, Elaine Heumann (1991): "Noodling around with exhibition opportunities", In Karp, Ivan & Lavine, Steven D. (eds.), *Exhibiting Cultures. The Poetics and Politics of Museum Display*. Washington-London: Smithsonian Institution Press, pp. 176–190.

Gurian, Elaine Heumann (2006): *Civilizing the Museum: The Collected Writings of Elaine Heumann Gurian*. London-New York: Routlege.

Guzin-Lukic, Nada (2017): "Muséologie critique: du musée prédateur au musée créateur", *The Predatory Museum: ICOFOM Study Series*, 45, pp. 117–119.

Hainard, Jacques (1987): "Pour une muséologie de la rupture", *Musées*, 10, pp. 44–46.

Halpin, Marjorie M (1997): "Play it again, Sam: Reflections on a new museology", *Museum International*, 49 (2) (April–June), pp. 52–56.

Hanáková, Petra (2005): "Teoretické koncepty kritickej muzeológie", *ARS*, 38 (1), pp. 20–22.

Hansen, Tone (2011): *(Re)Staging the Art Museum*. Berlin: Revolver Publishing.

Harris, Jennifer (2011): "Dialogism: The ideal and reality for museums", *ICOFOM Study Series*, 40, pp. 87–96.

Harris, Jonathan (2001): *The New Art History. A Critical Introduction*. Abingdon-New York: Routledge.

Harris, Neil (1995): "Museums and controversy. Some introductory reflections", *The Journal of American History*, 82 (3), pp. 1102–1110.

Harrison, Rodney (2013): *Heritage: Critical Approaches*. Abingdon: Routledge.

Hasian, Marouf & Wood, Rulon (2010): "Critical museology, (Post)colonial communication, and the gradual mastering of traumatic pasts at the Royal Museum for Central Africa (RMCA)", *Western Journal of Communication*, 74 (2) (marzo–abril), pp. 128–149.

Henning, Michelle (2006): *Museums, Media and Cultural Theory*. Maidenhead: Open University Press.

Hernández Hernández, Francisca (2006): *Planteamientos teóricos de la museología*. Gijón: Trea.

Hernández Hernández, Francisca (2015): "La Museología entre la tradición y la posmodernidad", *Complutum*, 26 (2), pp. 9–26.

Hernández Hernández, Francisca (2018): *Reflexiones museológicas desde los márgenes*. Gijón: Trea.

Hoff, Mónica (2019): "If the museum is a school, what kind of school are we talking about?" In Álvarez Moreno, Ekaterina (ed.), *Museología crítica: Temas selectos. Reflexiones de la Cátedra William Bullock/Critical Museology: Selected Themes. Reflections from the William Bullock Lecture Series*. Ciudad de México: MUAC, pp. 238–244.

Holo, Shelma R. (2019): "Representing belonging in the United States: Hyphenated or ethnically/culturally specific museums", In Álvarez Moreno, Ekaterina (ed.), *Museología crítica: Temas selectos. Reflexiones de la Cátedra William Bullock/Critical Museology: Selected Themes. Reflections from the William Bullock Lecture Series*. Ciudad de México: MUAC, pp. 304–317.

Holo, Shelma & Álvarez, Mari Tere (eds.), *Beyond the Turnstile: Making the Case for Museums and Sustainable Values*. Lanham-New York-Toronto-Plymouth: Altamira Press.

Honorato, Cayo (2014): "A formação do artista-educador, aproximadamente", In Chaud, E. (ed.), *Anais: VII Seminário Nacional de Pesquisa em Arte e Cultura Visual*. Goiânia, GO: UFG, FAV, pp. 522–532.

Hooper-Greenhill, Eilean (ed.) (1999): *Museum, Media, Message*. London: Routledge.

Hooper-Greenhill, Eilean (2000): *Museums and the Interpretation of Visual Culture*. London-New York: Routledge.

Hooper-Greenhill, Eilean (2007): "Interpretive communities, strategies and repertoires", In Watson, Sheila (ed.), *Museums and Their Communities*. New York: Routledge, pp. 76–94.

Houtmann, Gustaaf (2009): "Negotiating new visions. An interview with Anthony Shelton", *Anthropology Today*, 25 (6), pp. 7–13.

Janulardo, Ettore (2015): "Metamorfosi di architetture. Strutture ed esposizioni alla Centrale Montemartini di Roma", *BTA -Bollettino Telematico dell'Arte* (759). www.bta.it/txt/a0/07/bta00759.html.

Jenkins, Tiffany (2016): *Keeping their Marbles*. Oxford: Oxford University Press.

Karp, Ivan & Kratz, Corinne A. (2015): "The interrogative museum", In Silverman, Raymond A. (ed.), *Museum as Process: Translating Local and Global Knowledges*. London: Routledge, pp. 279–298.

Karp, Ivan, Kratz, Corinne A., Szwaja, Lynn & Ybarra-Frausto, Tomás (eds.) (2006): *Museum Frictions. Public Cultures/Global Transformations*. Durham-London: Duke University Press.

Karp, Ivan & Lavine, Steven D. (eds.) (1991): *Exhibiting Cultures. The Poetics and Politics of Museum Display*. Washington-London: Smithsonian Institution Press.

Kester, Grant H. (2004): *Conversation Pieces: Community and Communication in Modern Art*. Berkeley: University of California Press.

Kirshenblatt-Gimblett, Barbara (1991): "Objects of ethnography", In Karp, Ivan & Lavine, Steven D. (eds.), *Exhibiting Cultures. The Poetics and Politics of Museum Display*. Washington-London: Smithsonian Institution Press, pp. 386–443.

Kirshenblatt-Gimblett, Barbara (2015): "Historical Space and Critical Museologies: POLIN museum of the history of polish Jews", In Murawska-Muthesius,

Katarzyna & Piotrowski, Piotr (eds.), *From Museum Critique to the Critical Museum*. Farnham-Burlington: Ashgate, pp. 147–161.

Klausewitz, Wolfgang (1989): "Zur Geschichte der Museologie (1878–1988)", In Auer, Hermann (ed.), *Museologie. Neue Wege – Neue Ziele*. Munich-London-New York-Paris: Deutsches Nationalkomitee des Internationalen Museumsrates ICOM, pp. 20–37.

Klonk, Charlotte (2009): *Spaces of Experience: Art Gallery Interiors from 1800 to 2000*. New Haven-London: Yale University Press.

Knell, Simon (2016): *National Galleries. The Art of Making Nations*. London-New York: Routledge.

Knell, Simon (ed.) (2019): *The Contemporary Museum. Shaping Museums for the Global Now*. London-New York: Routledge.

Knell, Simon, MacLeod, Suzanne & Watson, Sheila (eds.) (2007) : *Museum Revolutions. How Museums Change and Are Changed*. London-New York: Routledge.

Kreps, Chistina (2006): "Non-Western models of museums and curation in cross-cultural perspective", In MacDonald, Sharon (ed.), *A Companion to Museum Studies*. Malden, MA-Oxford, Carlton: Blackwell, pp. 457–472.

Lahav, Sylvia (2000): "A special place/A learning space: Museums in the twenty-first century", *The Art Book*, 7 (4), pp. 20–24.

Lavine, Steven D. & Karp, Ivan (1991): "Museums and multiculturalism", In Karp, Ivan & Lavine, Steven D. (eds.), *Exhibiting Cultures. The Poetics and Politics of Museum Display*. Washington-London: Smithsonian Institution Press.

Lawrence, Amanda R. (2015): "Preservation through replication: The Barnes foundation", *Future Anterior*, 12 (1), pp. 1–15.

Lehrer, Erica T. (2016): "Public pedagogy and transnational, transcultural museums", In Grudzinska-Gross, Irena & Nawrocki, Iwa (eds.), *Poland and Polin: New Interpretations in Polish-Jewish Studies*. Frankfurt: Peter Lang, pp. 197–218.

Leite, Pedro Pereira (2012): *Olhares Biográficos: A poética da intersubjetividade em museologia*. Lisbon: Marca d'Agua.

Leshchenko, Anna (2009): "Проблемы становления музееведческой терминологии на международном уровне" (Problems of the formation of an international museum terminology). *Muzej*, 5, pp. 42–46.

Levin, Amy K. (ed.) (2010): *Gender, Sexuality and Museums: A Routledge Reader*. London: Routledge.

Lindsay, Georgia (2016): *The User Perspective on Twenty-First-Century Art Museums*. New York-London: Routledge.

Litwak, Jane Marie (1996): "Visitors learn more from labels that ask questions", *Current Trends in Audience Research and Evaluation*, 10, pp. 40–51.

Loeseke, Annette (2019): "Transhistoricism. Using the past to critique the present" In Knell, Simon (ed.), *The Contemporary Museum. Shaping Museums for the Global Now*. London-New York: Routledge, pp. 142–151.

Lord, B. (2005): "Representing Enlightenment space", In MacLeod, Suzanne (ed.), *Reshaping Museum Space. Architecture, Design, Exhibitions*. Abingdon: Routledge, pp. 146–157.

Lorente, Jesús-Pedro (2006): "Nuevas tendencias en teoría museológica: A vueltas con la museología crítica", *Museos.es* (2), pp. 24–33.

Lorente, Jesús Pedro (2011): "El multiculturalismo como piedra de toque en Canadá: los museos de Vancouver a la luz de la museología crítica", *HerMus: Heritage & Museography* (6), pp. 112–129. www.raco.cat/index.php/Hermus/article/view/313667/403780.

Lorente, Jesús Pedro (2012): "The development of museum studies in Universities: From technical training to critical museology", *Museum Management and Curatorship*, 27 (3) pp. 237–252.

Lorente, Jesús-Pedro (2013): "On the limits of institutional art criticism (and critical museology as established discourse)", *Art.es* (53), pp. 131–135.

Lorente, Jesús-Pedro (2014): "Mnemósine en el templo de las musas: La memoria (meta)museográfica y la historia de los museos", In Prieto, José y Ruiz, Vega (coords.), *Arte y Memoria. 2.* Teruel: Tervalis, pp. 107–117.

Lorente, Jesús-Pedro (2015): "From the white cube to a critical museography: The development of interrogative, plural and subjective museum discourses", In Murawska-Muthesius, Katarzyna & Piotrowski, Piotr (eds.), *From Museum Critique to the Critical Museum.* Farnham-Burlington: Ashgate, pp. 115–128.

Lorente, J. Pedro (2019): *Public Art and Museums in Cultural Districts.*, London-New York: Routledge.

Lorente, Jesús-Pedro (2021): "Avant-garde art display recreations historised: Muzeum Sztuki in Łódź as a referential case?" *Muzeológia a kultúrne dedičstvo*, 9 (3), pp. 5–15.

Lorente, Jesús Pedro (dir.) & Almazán, David (coord.) (2003): *Museología crítica y arte contemporáneo.* Saragossa: Prensas Universitarias de Zaragoza.

Lorente, Jesús-Pedro & Gómez Martínez, Javier (2021): "Miradas al/desde el museo del siglo XXI: (re)acoplamientos visuales con los distritos culturales circundantes", *Revista de Museología* (81) nº 82, p. 47–58.

Lorente, Jesús-Pedro & Moolhuijsen, Nicole (2015): "La muséologie critique: entre ruptures et réinterpretations", *La Lettre de L'OCIM* (158), pp. 19–24. https://ocim.revues.org/1495.

MacDonald, George F. & Alsford, Stephen (1995): "Canadian museums and the representation of culture in a multicultural nation", *Cultural Dynamics*, 7 (1), pp. 15–26.

MacDonald, Sharon (2003): "Museums, national and postnational and transcultural identities", *Museum and Society*, 1 (1), pp. 1–16.

MacDonald, Sharon (ed.) (2006): *A Companion to Museum Studies.* Malden, MA-Oxford: Blackwell.

MacDonald, Sharon & Basu, Paul (eds.) (2007): *Exhibition Experiments.* Oxford: Blackwell Publishers.

MacDonald, Sharon & Fyfe, Gordon (eds.) (1996): *Theorizing Museums: Representing Identity and Diversity in a Changing World.* Oxford: Blackwell Publishers.

MacLeod, Suzanne (ed.) (2005): *Reshaping Museum Space: Architecture, Design, Exhibitions.* London: Routledge.

Mairesse, François (2006): "L'histoire de la muséologie est-elle finie?¿Ha terminado la historia de la museología?" In: Viereg, Hildegard K., Risnicoff De Gorgas, Mónica, Schiller, Regina & Troncoso, Martha (eds.), *Museology – A Field of Knowledge. Museology and History/Museología: Un campo del conocimiento. Museología e Historia.* Munich-Alta Gracia: ICOFOM Study Series 35, pp. 86–102.

Mairesse, Francois (2015): "Museology at a crossroads", *Museologica Brunensia*, 4 (2), pp. 4–9.

Marcus, George E. & Fischer, Michael J. (1986): *Antropology as Cultural Critique: An Experimental Moment in the Human Sciences*. Chicago: University of Chicago Press.

Marín Torres, María Teresa (2003): "Territorio jurásico: de museología crítica e historia del arte en España", In Lorente, J. P (dir.) y Almazán, David (coord.), *Museología crítica y arte contemporáneo*. Saragossa: Prensas Universitarias de Zaragoza, pp. 27–50.

Maroevic, Ivo (1998): *Introduction to Museology: The European Approach*. Munich: Müller-Straten.

Marstine, Janet (ed.) (2006): *New Museum Theory and Practice: An Introduction*. London-Malden: Blackwell, pp. 1–37.

Marstine, Janet (2013): "Situated revelations: Radical transparency in the museum", In Marstine, Janet, Bauer, Alexander A. & Haines, Chelsea (eds.), *New Directions in Museum Ethics*. London: Routledge, pp. 1–23.

Marstine, Janet & Mintcheva, Svetlana (2021): *Curating Under Pressure. International Perspectives on Negotiating Conflict and Upholidng Integrity*. London-New York: Routledge.

Mason, Rhiannon (2006): "Cultural theory and museum studies", In Macdonald, S. (ed.), *A Companion to Museum Studies*. Oxford: Blackwell, pp. 17–32.

McClellan, Andrew (2008): *The Art Museum from Boullée to Bilbao*. Berkeley-Los Angeles-London: University of California Press.

McLuhan, Marshall, Parker, Harley & Barzun, Jacques (2008): *Le Musée non linéaire. Exploration des méthodes, moyens et valeurs de la communication avec le public par le musée*. Lyon: Aléas.

McShine, Kynaston (1999): *The Museum as Muse: Artists Reflect*. New York: The Museum of Modern Art.

Mensch, Peter van (1990): "Methodological museology; or, towards a theory of museum practice", In Pearce, S. (ed.), *Objects of Knowledge*. London-Atlantic Highlands: The Atholone Press, pp. 141–157.

Mensch, Peter van (1992): *Towards a Methodology of Museology*. Zagreb: University of Zagreb.

Mensch, Peter van (1996): "Museological research", In Mench, P. van (ed.), *Museological Research, ICOFOM Study Series*, 21, pp. 19–33.

Mensch, Peter van & Meijer-Van Mensch, Leontine (2015): *New Trends in Museology II*. Celje: Muzej novejše zgodovine.

Message, Kylie (2015): "Contentious politics and museums as contact zones", In Witcomb, Andrea & Message, Kylie (eds.), *The International Handbooks of Museum Studies: Museum Theory*. New York: John Wiley & Sons, pp. 253–281.

Message, Kylie (2018): *The Disobedient Museum. Writing at the Edge*. London-New York: Routledge.

Meszaros, Cheryl (2006): "Now that is evidence: Tracking down the evil 'whatever interpretation'", *Visitor Studies Today*, 9 (3), pp. 10–12.

Montaner, Josep Maria (2003): *Museos para el siglo XXI. Museums for the 21st Century*. Barcelona: Gustavo Gili.

Möntmann, Nina (ed.) (2006): *Art and Its Institutions: Current Conflicts, Critique and Collaborations*. London: Black Dog Pub Ltd.

Morales Moreno, Luis Gerardo (2007): "Vieja y nueva museología en México", In Bellido Gant, María Luisa (coord.), *Aprendiendo de Latinoamérica. El museo como protagonista*. Gijón: Trea, pp. 342–374.

Morales Moreno, Luis Gerardo (ed.) (2015): *Tendencias de la museología en América Latina. Articulaciones, horizontes, diseminaciones*. Ciudad de México: ENCRYM-INAH.

Morales Moreno, Luis Gerardo (2019): "Knowlede, ritual and enjoyment in museology", In Álvarez Moreno, Ekaterina (ed.), *Museología crítica: Temas selectos. Reflexiones de la Cátedra William Bullock/Critical Museology: Selected Themes. Reflections from the William Bullock Lecture Series*. Ciudad de México: MUAC, pp. 204–224.

Mouffe, Chantal (2013): "Institutions as sites of agonistic intervention", In Gielen, Pascal (ed.), *Institutional Attitudes. Instituting Art in a Flat World*. Amsterdam: Valiz, pp. 63–74.

Mupira, Paul (ed.) (2002): *Hot Spot: Awareness Making on Contemporary Issues in Museums*. Stockholm: Samp.

Murawska-Muthesius, Katarzyna & Piotrowski, Piotr (eds.) (2015): *From Museum Critique to the Critical Museum*. Farnham-Burlington: Ashgate.

Nashashibi, Salwa Mikdadi (2003): "Visitor voices in art museums: The visitor-written label", *Journal of Museum Education*, 28 (3), pp. 21–25.

Navajas Corral, Óscar (2020): *Nueva museología y museología social. Una historia narrada desde la experiencia española*. Gijón, Trea.

Navarro, Óscar (2012): "History and education as bases for museum legitimacy in Latin American museums: Some comments for a discussion from critical museology point of view", *Museologica Brunensia*, 1 (1), s. 28–33. ISSN: 1805–4722.

Navarro Rojas, Óscar (2006): "Museos y museología: Apuntes para una museología crítica", en *XXIX Congreso Anual del ICOFOM/XV Congreso Regional del ICOFOM-LAM: Museología e Historia: un campo de conocimiento*, Córdoba-Alta Gracia (Argentina), 5–15 octubre 2006. www.icofom-lam.org/files/museos_y_museologia_critica_-_copia_2.pdf.

Navarro Rojas, Óscar & Tsagaraki, Christina (2009/2010): "Museos en la crisis: una visión desde la museología crítica", *Museos.es*, 5–6, pp. 50–57.

Newhouse, Victoria (1998): *Towards a New Museum*. New York: Monacelli.

Nomikou, Effrosyni Nomikou (2015): "Museology without a prefix: Some thoughts on the epistemology and methodology of an integrated approach", *ICOFOM Study Series* (43a), pp. 203–215.

Noronha, Elisa (2017): *Discursos e reflexividade: um estudo sobre a musealização da arte contemporânea*. Oporto: Ediçoes Afrontamento-CITCEM.

O'Doherty, Brian (1986). *Inside the White Cube. The Ideology of the Gallery Space*. Santa Monica : Lapis Press.

O'Neill, Mark (2010): "Kelvingrove: Telling stories in a treasured old/new museum", *Curator The Museum Journal*, 50(4): 379–399.

O'Neill, Paul (2016): *The Culture of Curating and the Curating of Culture(s)*. Cambridge, MA: The MIT Press.

Orišková, Mária (ed.) (2006): *Efekt múzea: predmety, praktiky, publikum: Antoló-
gia textov anglo-americkej kritickej teórie múzea.* Bratislava: Vysoká škola výt-
varných umení.

Padró, Carla (2003): "La museología crítica como una forma de reflexionar sobre
los museos como zonas de conflicto e intercambio", In Lorente, J. Pedro (dir.) &
Almazán, David (coord.), *Museología crítica y arte contemporáneo.* Saragossa:
Prensas Universitarias de Zaragoza, pp. 51–70.

Padró, Carla (2010): "Una nueva opción: la museología crítica: Una opción a la
crítica que dio lugar a la nueva museología (y 'algo' de una práctica docente)",
En *Actas de los XX Cursos Monográficos sobre el Patrimonio Histórico:[Reinosa,
julio de 2009].* Santander: Servicio de Publicaciones de la Universidad de Cantabria, pp. 317–338.

Padró, Carla (2011): "Retos de la museología crítica desde la pedagogía crítica y
otras intersecciones", *Museo y Territorio,* 4, pp. 102–114.

Pagani, Camilla (2017): "Exposing the predator, recognising the prey: New institutional strategies for a reflexive museology", *ICOFOM Study Series,* 45, pp. 71–83.

Parramón, Ramón (2018): "Aesthetics of collaboration. Intermediations between
the collective, the participatory and the collaborative in systemic artistic practices", In Aramburu, Nekane (ed.), *D'ananda i tornada. Projectes i practiques
col.laboratives des del museu i a través de l'art.* Palma de Mallorca: Es Baluard
Museu d'Art Modern, pp. 180–187.

Patterson, Monica Eileen (2021): "Towards a critical chidren's museology: The any-
thing goes exhibition at the national museum in Warsaw", *Museum & Society,* 19
(3), pp. 330–350.

Phillips, Ruth B. (2003): "Community collaboration in exhibitions. Towards a dialogic paradigm", In Peers, L. & Brown, A. (eds.), *Museums and Source Communities: A Routledge Reader.* London-New York: Routledge, pp. 155–170.

Pieterse, J. N. (2005): "Multiculturalism and museums. Discourse about others in
the age of globalization", In Corsane, Gerard (ed.), *Heritage, Museums and Galleries. An Introductory Reader.* London-New York: Routledge, pp. 163–183.

Piotrowski, Piotr (2011): "Museum: From the critique of institution to a critical
institution", In Hansen, T. (ed.), *(Re)Staging the Art Museum.* Berlin: Revolver
Publishing, pp. 77–92.

Popadić, Milan (2020): "The beginnings of Museology", *Muzeológia a kultúrne
dedičstvo,* vol. 8, n. 25, p. 5–16.

Poulot, Dominique (2005): *Musée et muséologie.* Paris: La Découverte, reed. 2009.

Preziosi, Donald & Farago, Claire (eds.) (2004): *Grasping the World. The Idea of
the Museum.* Aldershot-Burlington, VT: Ashgate Press.

Psarra, Sophia (2009): *Architecture and Narrative. The Formation of Space and
Cultural Meaning.* New York: Routledge.

Putnam, James (2001): *Art and Artifact: The Museum as Medium.* London:
Thames & Hudson.

Rand, Steven & Kouris, Heather (eds.) (2007): *Cautionary Tales: Critical Curation.*
New York: Apexart.

Raunig, Gerard & Ray, Gene (2009): *Art and Contemporary Critical Practice: Reinventing Institutional Critique.* London: MayFlyBooks.

Rectanus, Mark W. (2020): *Museums Inside Out. Artist Collaborations and New Exhibitions Ecologies*. Minneapolis-London: University of Minnesota Press.

Rees Leahy, Helen (2012): "Making an exhibition of ourselves", In Hill, Kate (ed.), *Museums and Biographies. Stories, Objects, Identities*. Woodbridge: Newcastle University-The Boydell Press, pp. 145–155.

Reese, Elizabeth B. (2003): "Art takes me there: Engaging the narratives of community members through interpretative exhibition processes and programming", *Art Education*, 56 (1), pp. 33–39.

Rodney, Sheph (2019): *The Personalization of the Museum Visit. Art Museums, Discourse and Visitors*. London: Routledge.

Rodrigo, Javier (2007); *Pràctiques dialògiques: Interseccions de la pedagogia crítica i la museologia crítica. Prácticas dialógicas: Intersecciones entre la pedagogía crítica y la museología crítica. Dialogical Practices: Intersections between Critical Pedagogy and Critical Museology*. Palma de Mallorca: Es Baluard Museu d'Art Modern i contemporani de Palma.

Rodríguez Ortega, Núria (2011): "Discursos y narrativas digitales desde la perspectiva de la museología crítica", *Museo y Territorio*, 4, pp. 14–27.

Rogoff, Irit (2008): "Turning", *e-flux journal*, 11, pp. 1–10.

Roigé, Xavier (2007): "Museos etnológicos: entre la crisis y la redefinición", *Quaderns-e de l'ICA* (9), p. 8.

Rosof, Nancy (2003): "Integrating native views into museum procedures: Hope and practice at the National Museum of the American Indian", In Peers, Laura & Brown, Alison (eds.), *Museums and Source Communities*. London-New York: Routledge.

Sadurni Rodríguez, Núria (2014): "Curaduría educativa: ¿democratizar el espacio o ejercer el poder?" *Nierika, Revista de Estudios de Arte*, 6, pp. 35–48.

Sánchez, Sofía (2020): "El Mât de Molinos, peirón de la Nueva Museología", *AACA Digital*, 50.

Sandell, Richard & Nightingale, Eithne (eds.) (2012): *Museums, Equality, and Social Justice*. Abingdon, Oxon-New York: Routledge.

Santacana, Joan & Hernández Cardona, Francesc Xavier (2006): *Museología Crítica*. Gijón: Trea.

Schärer, Martin (2018): *Exposer la muséologie*. Paris: ICOFOM.

Schorch, Philipp (2013): "Contact zones, third spaces, and the act of interpretation", *Museum and Society*, 11 (1), pp. 68–81.

Schubert, Karsten (2000): *The Curator's Egg. The Evolution of the Museum Concept from the French Revolution to the Present Day*. London: One-Off Books.

Semedo, Alice (2020): "Border pedagogy and empowerment education in museums", In Alejandra ALONSO TAK & Ángel PAZOS-LÓPEZ (eds.), *Socializing Art Museums. Rethinking the Publics' Experience*. Berlin-Boston: De Gruyter, p. 107–142.

Semedo, Alice & Ferreira, Inês (2017): "Museus e Museologia: desafios para a construção de territórios colaborativos", *Sociologia: Revista da Faculdade de Letras da Universidade do Porto*, 21, pp. 97–119.

Serota, Nicholas (1996): *Experience or Interpretation. The Dilemma of Museums of Modern Art*. London: Thames & Hudson.

Sheehan, James J. (2000): *Museums in the German Art World from the End of the Old Regime to the Rise of Modernism*. Oxford: Oxford University Press.

Shelton, Anthony A. (1990): "In the lair of the monkey: Notes towards a post-modernist museography", In Pearce, Susan M. (ed.), *Objects of Knowledge*. London: The Athlone Press, pp. 78–102.

Shelton, Anthony A. (1992): "Constructing the global village", *Museums Journal* (August), pp. 25–26.

Shelton, Anthony A. (2001): "Unsettling the meaning: Critical museology, art, and anthropological discourse", In Bouquet, Mary (ed.), *Academic Anthropology and the Museum*. Oxford-New York: Berghahn Books, pp. 142–161.

Shelton, Anthony A. (2013): "Critical museology. A Manifesto", *Museum Worlds Advances in Research*, 1 (1), pp. 7–23.

Sherman, Daniel J. & Rogoff, Irit (eds.) (1994): *Museum Culture: Histories, Discourses, Spectacles*. London: Routledge.

Simon, Nina Simon (2010): *The Participatory Museum*. Santa Cruz, CA: Museum 2.0.

Simpson, Moa (1996): *Making representations. Museums in the Post-colonial Era*. London: Routledge.

Smart, William (2020): "The Open and Integrated Museum", In Lindsay, Georgia (ed.), *Contemporary Museum Architecture and Design*. New York-London: Routledge, pp. 137–154.

Smith, Charles Samaurez (2007): "Narratives of display at the national gallery, London", *Art History*, 30 (4), pp. 611–627.

Smith, Laurajane (2012): *All Heritage is Intangible. Critical Heritage Studies and Museums*. Amsterdam: Reinwardt Academy.

Smith, Terry (2012): *Thinking Contemporary Curating*. New York: Independent Curators International.

Sola Pizarro, Belén (2019): *Exponer o exponerse: la educación en museos como producción cultural crítica*. Madrid: Catarata.

Sompairac, Arnaud (2016): *Scénographie d'exposition: Six Perspectives Critiques*. Geneva: MétisPresses.

Stam, Deirdre C. (1993): "The informed muse: The implications of 'the new museology' for museum practice", *Museum Management and Curatorship*, 12 (3), pp. 267–283.

Tali, Margaret (2018): *Absence and Difficult Knowledge in Contemporary Art Museums*. New York-London: Routledge.

te Heesen, Anke (2012): *Theorien des Museums zur Einführung*. Hamburg: Junius Verlag.

Teather, Lynne (1984): *Museology and Its Traditions. The British Experience, 1845–1945*. PhD Thesis, University of Leicester, Department of Museum Studies. https://leicester.figshare.com/articles/thesis/Museology_and_its_traditions_The_British_experience_1845-1945_/10157582.

Teather, Lynne (1991): "Museum studies. Reflecting on reflective practice", *Museum Management and Curatorship*, 10, pp. 403–417.

Teather, Lynne (2009): "Mapping museologies: From babel tower to borderlands", In Dolák, J. (ed.), *Museology at the Beginning of the 3rd Millennium*. Brno: Technicke´ Muzeum v Brne, pp. 75–96.

Teather, Lynne (2012): "Museum studies borderlands: Negotiating curriculum and competencies", *Cadernos de Sociomuseologia*, 43, pp. 63–102.

Teather, Lynne & Carter, Jennifer (2009): "Critical museology now: Theory/practice/theory", *Muse*, XXVII (6), pp. 22–33.

Tejeda Martín, I. (2012): "La copia y la reconstrucción: un recurso visual en las exposiciones de arte moderno desde los años 60 del siglo XX", *Arte, Individuo y Sociedad*, 24 (2), pp. 211–226.

Toon, Richard (2007) "Science centres. A museum studies approach to their development and possible future direction", en KNELL, Simon, MacLEOD, Suzanne & WATSON, Sheila (eds.) (2007). *Museum Revolutions. How Museums change and are Changed,* London-New York : Routledge, pp. 105–116.

Troelenberg, Eva-Maria & Savino, Melania (2017): *Images of the Art Museum. Connecting Gaze and Discourse in the History of Museology.* Berlin-Boston: De Gruyter.

Tzortzi, Kali (2015): *Museum Space: Where Architecture meets Museology.* Abingdon-New York, Ashgate.

Van Geert, Fabien (2018): "Le Musée d'ethnographie de Neuchâtel, Suisse. Vers une muséologie de la pensé. L'expérience du Musée d'ethnographie de Neuchâtel", In Garcin-Marrou, Flore, Mairesse, François & Mouton-Rezzouk, Aurélie (eds.), *Des lieux pour penser. Musées, théâtres, bibliothèques. Matériaux pour une discussion.* Paris: ICOM-ICOFOM, pp. 286–290.

Vergo, Peter (ed.) (1989): *The New Museology.* London: Reaktion Books.

Waltz, Markus (2018): *"The German Voice in the "Babelian Tale of Museology and Museography": Creation and Use of Terms for Museum Science in Germany, Museologica Brunensia,* 7 (2), pp. 5–18.

Warner, Michael (2002): *Publics and Counterpublics.* Cambridge: Zone Books.

Wastiau, Boris (2002): "La reconversion du musée glouton", In Gonseth, Marc-Olivier, Hainard, Jacques & Kaer, Roland (eds.), *Le Musée cannibale.* Neuchâtel: MEN, pp. 85–109.

Watson, Sheila (ed.) (2007): *Museums and Their Communities.* New York: Routledge.

Watson, Sheila (2015): "Emotions in the history museum", In Witcomb, Andrea & Message, Kylie (eds.), *The International Handbooks of Museum Studies: Museum Theory.* New York: John Wiley & Sons, pp. 288–301.

Welchman, John C. (ed.) (2006): *Institutional Critique and After.* Zurich-Los Angeles: JRP-Ringier- The Southern California Consortium of Art Schools.

Welsh, Peter H. (2005): "Re-configuring museums", *Museum Management and Curatorship*, 20, pp. 103–130.

Whitehead, Christopher (2005): "Visiting with suspicion. Recent perspectives on art museums and galleries", In Corsane, Gerard (ed.), *Heritage, Museums and Galleries. An Introductory Reader.* London-New York: Routledge, pp. 89–101.

Whitehead, Christopher (2012a): *Interpreting Art in Museums and Art Galleries.* London-New York: Routledge.

Whitehead, Christopher (2012b): "Institutional autobiography and the architecture of the art museum: Restoration and remembering at the National Gallery in the 1980s", In Hill, Kate (ed.), *Museums and Biographies. Stories, Objects, Identities.* Woodbridge: Newcastle University-The Boydell Press, pp. 157–170.

Winter, Tim (2012): "Clarifying the critical in critical heritage studies", *International Journal of Heritage Studies*, 19 (6), pp. 532–545.

Witcomb, Andrea (2003): *Re-Imagining the Museum: Beyond the Mausoleum*. London-New York: Routledge.

Witcomb, Andrea (2015): "Toward a pedagogy of feeling. Understanding how museums create a space for cross-cultural encounters", In Witcomb, Andrea & Message, Kylie (eds.), *The International Handbooks of Museum Studies: Museum Theory*. New York: John Wiley & Sons, pp. 321–344.

Witcomb, Andrea & Buckley, Kristal (2013): "Engaging with the future of 'critical heritage studies': Looking back in order to look forward", *International Journal of Heritage Studies*, 19 (6), pp. 562–578.

Wittocx, Eva, et al. (2018): *The Transhistorical Museum. Mapping the Field*. Amsterdam: Valiz.

Zuliani, Stefania (2009): *Effetto museo: Arte, critica, educazione*. Turin: Bruno Mondadori.

Index

Note: Page locators in *italics* indicate a figure on the corresponding page.

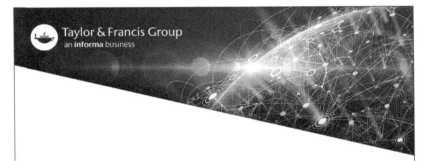

Printed and bound by CPI Group (UK) Ltd, Croydon, CR0 4YY
08/06/2025
01897001-0009